REGIONALISM:

The Caribbean Prospective

MARKIE SPRING

REGIONALISM:
The Caribbean Prospective

Order this book online at www.trafford.com
or email orders@trafford.com

Most Trafford titles are also available at major online book retailers.

Printed in the United States of America.

ISBN: 978-1-4269-5109-1 (sc)
ISBN: 978-1-4269-5110-7 (e)

Trafford rev. 05/17/2012

 www.trafford.com

North America & International
toll-free: 1 888 232 4444 (USA & Canada)
phone: 250 383 6864 ♦ fax: 812 355 4082

To the leaders of the Caribbean nations that have fought tirelessly to bring the region together - to the governing bodies of the other nations, your cooperation and compromise are inevitable for the success of the new regional strategy

Also by Markie Spring

Remnants of Faith

CONTENTS

Author's Note ix

Acknowledgement xiv

Prologue xvii

Part 1   The Caribbean 1

Part 2   Sports 27

Part 3   Tourism 69

Part 4   Safety and Security 109

Part 5   Politics 141

Part 6   Culture 183

Part 7   Education 217

Part 8   Economy 249

Part 9   Development 283

Epilogue:Strength Through Unity 307

Author's Note

The idea for this book originated out of many challenges, which exist amongst our islands in the Caribbean. Initially, my attention was focus on Cuba and its Communistic regime – the brutal family business, which exists there. Because, the Cubans instigated the 1983 overthrowing of the Grenadian democratic government, it has become a priority watch in my life. Hitherto, there are many issues confronting the Caribbean, which are only highlighted to make headline news across the region. After all, our leaders are not addressing these issues enough and this is the reason for this book; to wake up our leaders and have them confront these issues head-on.

A huge part of this book was taken from the media across the Caribbean and hundreds of conversations held with citizens of the West Indies. There were telephone debates, which lasted for hours between Ennis Grant and I. Ennis Grant is an academia who I respect for his intellect and knowledge about these issues. Also, Jasmine Alexander who discussed these issues with me on MSN messenger and in her comfy living room.

I must highlight that throughout these debates there were enormous disagreements of view points from varying citizens from around the Caribbean. One thing that was common is that more than eighty percent of the people rejected regionalism – people who cannot think outside the box. There point of views suggests that they are too individualistic in their thinking and purported that some Caribbean nations are superior to others.

After listening to so many people and sometimes engaged in heated debates, I have no other choice than wanting to run for office in St Vincent and the Grenadines in an effort to extend this idea throughout the Caribbean. First, I must sell his idea to the citizens of all the nations; I could make awareness through this simple title.

In essence, the people who want the changes are mostly those from the Eastern Caribbean Member States including a large number of Barbadians who liked the idea.

Some people from the larger islands crippled the new movement and indicated that they won't consider supporting the change.

Here, I employ all Caribbean nations to capture this moment and consider the benefits of regionalism in the West Indies. If our citizens are not sure then we must break it down to them and this is the reason for the existence of this book.

Hereafter, my quest is to get involved in politics in the Caribbean. I do not only want to limit my political career to St Vincent and the Grenadines, but to have my voice heard around the region. However, the idea is to start as a politician on a local basis and, thereafter spread my practice.

Three years from now when I hope to run for office in St Vincent and the Grenadines I wish to change the political system in the St Vincent and the Grenadines and moreover, the wider Caribbean. Too often, the politicians forget about the purpose of running for office; therefore, I wish to address these issues that are facing the country and for that matter the nations across the region.

Insidious, suspenseful, desolate and vituperative are ways in which I would describe the political environment in St Vincent and the Grenadines, and for that matter, the wider Caribbean. It is wistful to know that politicians have changed the true meaning of politics. Ideally, I see politics as a practice of government and managing of public affairs.

I believe in changing the *status quo* especially when there is deliberate ambiguity. I would like to see advertisement through mass media: television, radio, Internet and town hall meetings, rather than the conventional motorcade through towns and villages, which have, in the past, created problems.

In my quest for regionalism, I hope to address the economical, social and political factors, which often affects us as a nation - not only in St Vincent and the Grenadines, but the entire Caribbean.

Lastly, let me again highlight the case of the European Union. The Caribbean leaders and citizens alike might be of the opinion that some countries are too poor to integrate, but this is the real reason why we should integrate in an effort to strengthen our political, social economic environment.

Some European nation, especially those in Eastern Europe are not economically viable, but the regionalization process has caused the countries to developed initiatives where they were weak, hence, their success.

Acknowledgement

The author of this book would like to thank all those who shared their views about Caribbean integration, whether positive or negative. In our debates I learnt many things from them including what can't and what could be regionalized.

I would also like to extend my deepest appreciation to all of my colleagues for their intellectual depth and insight regarding the integration of the Caribbean nations. They believe that the region could integrate in many ways and gave me their support and convinced me from a Caribbean point-of-view.

I also recognize Ennis Grant of the Royal Turks and Caicos Islands Police Force for his prospective and the strategies the region should adapt through economical, political and social factors.

Thanks to a few classmates from Saint Mary's University for their support - who believe in me and encouraged me along the way. Special thanks to Sarah Dupre in St Lucia for endorsing that the Caribbean needs to become a single unit.

I cannot go on without mention Ingrid De La Cruz from the Dominican Republic for her support of taking care of our son Marcos when I am burning the midnight oil to make this second book a reality. Marcos is growing up quickly and I cherish each day I spent with him.

In addition, many citizens from various Caribbean Islands have shared their thoughts on the idea that purported that it would not work. From these feedbacks, it allowed me to highlight some of the challenges, which the leaders and citizens alike would face in the planning and implementation stages. The outstanding persons here are Ms. Monique Pinder, a nurse from Nassau, Bahamas, Ms. Jasmine Alexander, a teacher from St Vincent and the Grenadines, Ms. Joan Liburd from St Kitts and Nevis, and a few

Jamaican nationals that have implied that integrating the Caribbean would not be a success.

Hitherto, Ronald Landy and distinguished employee at Beaches resort, villages and spa in Turks and Caicos who believe that the Caribbean should integrate their efforts in all aspect. He believes that the region, operating as individual units will not prosper; instead the region would continue to experience declined growth in all aspects.

Prologue

Scattered like emeralds on the seas the Caribbean is paradise on earth - secluded, dazzling coral reefs, clear pristine waters and breath-taking cliffs are only some features of these exclusive islands.

Seeking an identity of its own like any other regions around the world, the Eastern Caribbean along with the Greater Antilles once form their own alliance to remove themselves from the cruel condition faced under British and other European control.

They form the Federation of the West Indies. This federation did not last long enough to gain any substantive progress in becoming a single independent state from European rule.

This could be the fact the each island, mainly the more developed countries of the Caribbean, see themselves as independent nations that could survive on its own; therefore they were not willing to compromise. Furthermore, some countries engaged in conflicts over economic policies. It has been fifty two years since the introduction of the failed federation.

The leaders of the Eastern Caribbean and the Greater Antilles should be applauded for this early vision, which the new governing bodies failed to take advantage of.

However, the predecessors of the 1958 leaders have established many other regional institutions in an effort to integrate the Caribbean with little progress and cooperation from the region body. Some of the other institutions that were created include CARICOM, Organization of Eastern Caribbean States and the Association of Caribbean States.

The introduction of the Caribbean Single Market Economy has sparked much controversy within the region; specifically, when Barbados stalled the progress of the movement by opting to change its immigration policies, which is contrary to what the single market project highlighted.

I realize that this movement would be a painstaking and sophisticated one, with great efforts and negotiation and many years of planning. I have foreseen many economic, social and political difficulties to conquer before we realized our goal ahead.

Much negotiation would have to be made with the Communist states of Cuba. The region would have to find way to deal with Cuba, or simply eliminate them until they change their political system.

This is in no way for me to extend our ideology on the people of Cuba, but to get in line with the political system of the majority Caribbean. The world has watch Communism and Socialism crumble in every nation which adapts this form of political system.

In light of all these challenges and the slow progress forward I felt obligated to write about it.

This book is influenced by the many challenges we are facing in the Caribbean today. Our unfixed financial problem is a continuous one, which is weakening by the hour. From Haiti, Jamaica, Guyana to the Dominican Republic there are evidence unnoticed.

As a result of these economic instabilities, unemployment in the Caribbean is constantly rising; forcing countries like those mentioned above to migrate to other islands in the region with sustainable economies, and international destinations including the United States, Canada and England.

The political arena is soaring to higher heights – the Cuban Communist regimes, the British take over in the Turks and Caicos Islands and the many social, economical and political issues within the region.

The level of sports played in the West Indies is not competitive enough to surpass other countries on the sporting world. Australia dominate cricket, Europe and South America are the front runners in soccer and United States dominate almost all other sports. The Caribbean is nowhere close to being the best in any sporting activity, except for Jamaica's recent success at the Beijing Olympics games in China.

Conversely, our cultures are rapidly diminishing from the many influences by the United States, particular by the Hip Hop culture. Our European oriented way of life is deteriorating. It is evident in the architecture of our cities and family houses to the music, which we listen to.

In fact, it is also reflecting in our education system where the region's governments are adapting the American school system. The change in the way we worship is evidence of the United States influence in the region. Jehovah Witness is widely spread across the Caribbean – a millenarian Christian denomination founded by a Restoration Minister from Pennsylvania, United States.

I realized the problems that each islands in the Caribbean are facing and I also know that there are many challenges to confront on the idea of regionalizing the Caribbean. However, I believe that the region could be more competitive on all fronts, only when they integrate into one unit.

My argument here is that the region, if remain individual units, will keep deteriorating in all aspects. Let me stress that the Bahamas is doing well, because of the millions of tourists that travel to those islands. Its location close to the United States has placed them in an ideal position to attract more tourist than other islands that are farther away. Its small population and the many inhabited islands allow the government there to save money on infrastructure, education and other institutions, coupled with the their ability to market the islands.

What I have noticed is that the countries in the region that proclaimed to be the More Developed Countries are currently the poorest and these are the nations that are failing to compromise and negotiate with the so called Lesser Developed Countries.

This view is the basis for the book – the strategies the Caribbean should develop, so that the region could be a better place to live, study and work in. This does not mean that everything will run smoothly, but there is no failure without a trial and without a trial we would never know whether the integration strategy would work.

It is time for us to model the United States and Europe in the way they made integration worked. Both regions have encountered enormous challenges and are still encountering problem, however, it is safe to say that most of these challenges have been accessed and overcome by constant mentoring, researching and the implementation of effective strategies.

Other than observing the environments in the Caribbean, the United States and Europe, I have offered my own opinion on the way things should be. I must stress that these opinions are personal and to some extend from a Vincentian point-of-view. These strategies might not be accurate, but it is the job of the leaders to compare and access all the information I have gathered over the years and presented in this book.

Additionally, I have mastered economics at a tertiary institution, therefore, I have utilized my ability to think and construct new ideas about this topic.

To be more précised, let me outline the organization of each chapter. The first part, I give a sense of where we are geographically, how our islands are constructed demographically, and the status of the region before and after the Europeans and the impact thereafter. The proceeding part discusses how sports could potentially combine the islands, as it did before when the West Indies cricket team dominated the cricketing world. It also implies where we have failed in sports and how we could enhance our competitiveness on the global stage. In the third part, I debate the importance of associating the travel industry within the region rather than competing against ourselves, and how we could implement this strategy. The next part reflects on the safety and security of the region. It shows how a Regional Police force could be mobilized into multiple societies simultaneously. Part five describes the political environment of the region; stressing extensively on the Communistic situation in

Cuba and the democratic type governance of the rest of the Caribbean nations. The sixth part of this book indicates that our behaviors derived from European, African and native Indians influences. These behaviors are evident in our music, food, languages and religious beliefs. Part seven discusses the important of education and the need to introduce more technical programs and faculties in our Universities. It also encourages parents, governments and organizations and companies to provide education to citizens, and research into advanced programs. The final part of this book refers to economic policies and regulations, which would be of ultimate importance in integrating the Caribbean. The various economic conditions of the islands are highlighted. There are many factors discussed in this part, such as agriculture, a monetary union, budget, competition and the need for a single market and widespread infrastructural development across the region.

Fundamentally, the strategies in ensuring that the Caribbean is fully integrated are backed by some facts, which governed the integration of the United States and Europe. The aim here is to benchmark these two regions to assist in eliminating potential conflicts.

Let me preclude that some of the facts provided might not be entirely accurate; therefore, I can be held accountable for any miss-communication.

Moreover, some nations of the Caribbean and around the world might not agree with my opinion, vision and strategies in regionalizing the Caribbean, therefore, I am prepared to be constructively criticized for my opinion and how I see the forward movement of the region, through my own eyes. Nevertheless, I hold firm the facts I presented and adamant in my beliefs.

It is in my own interest to persuade the citizens of the region to access and analyze the information in this book and weigh them against the past, current and future conditions of the region and the status of the two regions I have admired in the quest for oneness - the United States and the European Union.

Furthermore, some citizens within the Caribbean argued that too many Caribbean economies are too weak to have successful integration. Let me remind the public that the only countries in the European Union, which are economically vibrant, are those located in Western Europe. To date the European Union combined boasts the world's largest GDP-gross domestic product.

It is my view that no single Caribbean Island can survive on its own. Some nation's economic situation might seem enticing now, but the worst is yet to come. No individual island possesses enough resources to stand on its own. Additionally, some countries' economy is not diverse enough to secure independent and continuous growth; hence, my quest for regionalism.

~ **Part 1** ~

The Caribbean

Before Europeans came to the west, the Caribbean was a peaceful tropical paradise nestled in clean turquoise waters with lust green mountains and valleys, and vegetations scattered across small communities; coupled with the abundance foods and water on most of the islands.

For one to support regionalism in the Caribbean one has to first assess its environment – the past and present in an effort to make a way into the future.

The first nation in the West Indies with human existence was Cuba and Hispaniola-the present day Haiti and the Dominican Republic. The Casirimoid people were connected to edge grinding – a culture similar to the Archaic Aged Central America – they existed back to 4500 BC. This culture existed on the mainland Trinidad, Trinidad and Tobago.

Life then existed in the Lesser Antilles, specifically Antigua, Antigua and Barbuda then the Windward islands.

At the time the Europeans arrived to the New World Amerindians indigenous peoples lived on most of the islands. The Taino already were inhabitants of the Greater Antilles, inside the Bahamas and the Leeward Islands chain and the Caribs and Galibi lived in the Windward Islands.

History indicated that Christopher Columbus discovered these islands in the fifteenth century. Although this is not entirely true, Christopher Columbus having met the Carib, nomadic sea-faring tribes here, I believe that Spanish explorer had visited the islands. Consequently, many Caribbean native in their own version, identify these voyages to be a rediscovery.

More so, it has long been disputed that Christopher Columbus when he visited the new world, had first landed on San Salvador, an Island in the Southern Bahamas chain. Other natives of the Turks and Caicos Islands teach that the Spanish lead voyage to the New World first landed on the Island of Grand

Turk, the seven square mile island and capital of the Turks and Caicos Islands.

This new development has created academic disputes between the educators of the Bahamas and these of the Turks and Caicos Islands.

When Columbus set sail with his three ships in 1492, he believed that he had reached the southern part of India, therefore, he name the islands the West Indies. He named Caribbean Sea after the Carib people who were found on the islands, hence, the Caribbean is formally part of the West Indies.

Once the rest of Europe heard about the new world there was an influx of Europeans to the West Indies in search of new development and institutions.

Since the arrival of the Christopher Columbus and the European mainly the Spaniards, British, Dutch and French, the Caribbean has been struggling with the advent of European powers that left a scar on these secluded islands.

The British and French have raged several wars for the islands. The Europeans even fought against the native Indians over land space. These Europeans acknowledged that there were tremendous potentials especially in the Agriculture sectors.

Throughout the colonial history of the Caribbean, the European raged many minor wars. Some of these wars were a result of political agitation in the region.

There were the Thirty Years War between the Netherlands Antilles and Spain. The first, second and third Anglo-Dutch wars were fought in an effort to gain supremacy. This was a military conflict between England and the Dutch Republic lasting a couple of years when the Royal Navy joined forces with France against the Dutch Republic. Although the Anglo-Dutch wars were not fought on Caribbean soils, they affected the Caribbean greatly, because of the European presence in the West Indies.

Other wars fought both in Europe and in the region. The significant ones to name include the Nine Years War raged between many European powers during this time.

The War of Spanish Succession, a war fought amongst several European powers against the Kingdom of France. Moreover, the Seven Years War when Britain fought against France and Spain, in which the British defeated the French and its ally. Subsequent to this war, France surrendered Canada to the British and kept a few Islands in the Caribbean that was making many revenues on sugar plantations. Simultaneously, Britain had seized Havana and later traded the city for the entire state of Florida in the United States.

Also the French Revolution, which created an environment of political and social disorder and fundamental change in France's history. It is this period that enables Haiti to become an independent state - the first in the western hemisphere.

The American Revolution also sparked changes within political and social arenas in the Caribbean. Political agitation of the British colonies rejected the governing of the British parliament. This influenced battles between France and Great Britain amongst Caribbean nations, thus, America gained its independence through French Victories in the Caribbean.

Lastly, the Spanish-American War, military conflict, which was contested between the United States and Spain. As a result Spanish dominance in Cuba and Puerto Rico was defeated by the United States, hence, the Americans gained control over the two once Spanish Islands.

Hitherto, Cuba gained its independence in 1962 and Puerto Rico, to date, remained an unincorporated territory of the United States.

Colonialism in the West Indies has a profound impact on the modern territories of the islands and their societies.

Once Christopher Columbus communicated back to Spain that the islands were agriculturally potential, other European nation would explore the new world for sugar development. This agricultural dependency has created a change in the potentials of the financial environment of the Caribbean when these European powers implemented the plantation system. Furthermore, the West Indies became a significant colony during the eighteenth century when Britain imports on sugar was enormous. The goal here was to fill those gaps, or provide resources to European countries, which were not readily available there. At home, the British did not worry about paying wages in sugar production; hence, they enslaved Africans in the region to work on their sugar plantation at no cost. But slavery was abolished in the proceeding century therefore, a wage system was introduced. There is no reason to ask the question, why Western Europe are so economically vibrant?

The British strategy was to employ a number of unskilled workers to perform repetitive and monotonous tasks in an effort to avoid these workers from becoming efficient. In this capacity, they were not given the opportunity to learn other skills. As a result this move gave rise to low wages with little or no opportunity for growth.

More so, economical exploitation had left the region with a large number of unskilled labor force – only capable of performing tasks relating to the Agriculture Sector. In fact, this exploitation left the region with minimal capital for investments into other industries. Meanwhile the Europeans were enjoying and securing sustained economies and developing technologies superior to the rest of the world around them.

During the twentieth century many parts of the region had gained their independence, specifically from Britain, France, Spain and the Netherlands. Most of the countries gained their independence in the 1960's – Jamaica, the Bahamas, Barbados and Trinidad and Tobago to name a few and during the 1970's – Grenada, St Lucia, Dominica and St Vincent and the Grenadines amongst many more.

Antigua and Barbuda and St Kitts and Nevis gained their independence in early 1980's.

The Dominican Republic gained its independence in 1844. The Dominican Republic was once governed by Spain and then neighboring Haiti for a period of time.

This region became an important location during World War II and the post war periods.

It is here many African nationals were exploited through slavery

The triangular trade was introduced because of the demand for slaves to cultivate sugarcane and other crops.

The Europeans' goal was to expand and trade within the Caribbean, hence, the establishment of colonies within the region. The indigenous peoples were mostly peaceful Tainos and warlike Caribs who eat the people they defeated. The Caribs were too aggressive to be made into slaves; therefore, they were brutally decimated by the European settlers.

Subsequently, only a trace of this native community exists, only in Dominica and St Vincent and the Grenadines.

There is evidence of remnants of European ruins in all parts of the region - from the British cannons to the architecture of the buildings and landscapes.

Some islands are still dependent on these European countries that have colonized the regions for centuries - Anguilla, Turks and Caicos Islands, Cayman Islands, Virgin Islands and Montserrat, and the Netherland Antilles.

Other countries have fought tirelessly for their independence and were successful.

Much of the history in the region mirrored the traditional food, culture, religion, language and music.

The Caribbean is a region consists of the many islands and cays, as much as seven thousand and the Caribbean Sea. Geopolitically, the region is often labeled as the sub-region of the Americas, which consists of twenty seven territories, including dependencies, sovereign states, and departments. These parsley developed islands is located between Florida in the United States and Venezuela in South America. The islands stretched from the Bahamas in the north to Trinidad and Tobago in the south - just miles off Venezuela. However, the Bahamas sometimes remotely distinguished themselves from the rest of the Caribbean.

Its member states include of fifteen sovereign states - Guyana, Trinidad and Tobago, Grenada, St Vincent and the Grenadines, St Lucia, Dominica, Antigua and Barbuda, St Kitts and Nevis, Jamaica, Haiti, the Dominican Republic, the Bahamas, Cuba and Barbados; dependencies comprising of the Turks and Caicos Islands, British and United States Virgin Islands, Anguilla, Montserrat, Cayman Islands and the Netherlands Antilles; and departments of France, which are composed of Martinique, Guadeloupe, St Martin and St Bath.

Most of the islands are surrounded by the rough gigantic swells of the Atlantic Ocean on the right and the calm serine waters of the Caribbean Sea on the left - the exceptions being the Bahamas, Turks and Caicos Islands and Barbados that are not washed by the Caribbean Sea. These islands are surrounded by the Atlantic Ocean.

Moreover, the geography and climate of the regions varies, some islands like Dominica, St Vincent and the Grenadines, Hispaniola, Guadeloupe, Martinique, Grenada and Jamaica possess rugged terrains and volcanic origins, while other islands have relatively flat terrains. These include Antigua and Barbuda, Turks and Caicos Islands, Barbados, Aruba and the Cayman islands with no features of volcanic activities, but limestone soils.

The sizes of each island also vary. The largest being Cuba, with over forty thousand square miles to the smallest islands of a few acres in size.

The topography of the islands clearly determines the climate of the region. The entire region is tropical; however, rainfall varies according to size, water current and elevation.

Most of the islands possess huge tropical rain forests, which attract many inches of rain through out the year, whereas some islands are dry and arid with no running water.

Some countries are affected by warm and moist trade winds, which create rainforest in mountainous countries like Dominica and St Vincent and the Grenadines.

Northeast trade winds irregularly affected the northern islands during winter seasons from the warm environment.

Not withholding that many whales travel to the warm waters of the Atlantic Ocean to mate, during the winter period. Many schools of fish, and there marine lives migrated to the Caribbean Sea.

The Panama Canal also connects the Caribbean Sea to the Pacific Ocean, which makes shipping routes more accessible from the eastern world to the Caribbean region.

The demographics also vary. The entire population of the region is almost thirty seven millions people - the most populous island being Cuba having more than eleven million people. Some islands in the region have as low as two hundred people.

Conversely, the total land area of the combined islands is approximately one hundred thousand square miles.

The majority of people living on these islands are of African descents, with a remaining of Caribs Europeans, East Indians, Portuguese and a mixture of all ethnic groups. Lately, influxes of Syrians and Chinese immigrants have settled in the region.

Before the European arrived in the New World there were many indigenous people living on the islands. In addition, these tribes had their own languages and cultures. These tribes include the Arawak, Ciboney, Lucayan, Taino and Garifuna.

The countries of the Greater Antilles have far more people than the Lesser Antilles. The reason for this huge population concentration is that the Greater Antilles are more developed and attracted many other Caribbean nations who were seeking jobs. Furthermore, the Greater Antilles are far bigger than the islands of the Lesser Antilles. Nowadays, the population of the Greater Antilles is restricted by visa requirements to other countries. However, because of more sustained economies the ease of getting a visa to travel to other countries, the Lesser Antilles are less populated.

Some counties in the Caribbean claimed that there are more people living in other part of the globe, specifically the United States, Canada and the United Kingdom, than living at home.

Nationals from the Turks and Caicos Islands are leaving home for Miami and other parts of the United States while nationals from other Caribbean Islands are migrating to those islands.

The dependent territories and the some overseas departments are experiencing enormous immigration to their shores. Trends show that these countries have more employment opportunities than the bigger and more developed countries in the region – Cayman Islands, US and British Virgin Islands, and St Martin and St Maarten. Coupled to this, is the presence of the US dollar in these islands.

In an effort to join the Region of the Caribbean certain criteria must be met - defined by some form of regional institution. This institution must encourage stable democratic regimes and at the same time avoid human rights violations and work in line with rules and laws of a democratic system. More so, an economy that is effective, efficient and competitive should be one of the criteria; and one that is willing to operate according to the rules, policies and laws enacted by the regional institution.

Members who find it difficult to cope with the set laws may withdraw its membership status will be guided by policy and procedures.

These are better known by significant activities, which occurred during history or some natural resources, which the islands possess.

Jamaica is known as the land of wood and water, because of the many rivers and forestation of the four thousand square miles island.

Dominica is better described as the land of many rivers; the country having three hundred and sixty five rivers. Various Caribbean national often joke about being able to bathe in a different river each day of the year.

Similarly, Antigua and Barbuda that have three hundred and sixty five beaches - we joke in a similar way about visiting a different beach each day of the year.

Spice Island Grenada is known for the many spices grown there - cinnamon, nutmegs and clove.

Trinidad and Tobago has a large Hummingbird population with various species, hence, the name - Land of the Hummingbirds.

St Vincent and the Grenadines is simply called the land of the blessed and St Lucia the Helen of the West.

Like the rest of the world the Caribbean host a number of High Mountain peaks. Some of the highest elevations are Pico Duarte with more than ten thousand feet in height. The Loma Alto de la Bandera is more than nine thousand feet. Both mountain peaks are located in the Dominican Republic.

Other large mountain peaks rise to the sky in Countries such as Haiti, Dominica, St Vincent and the Grenadines and St Kitts and Nevis possess peaks ranging from three thousand feet to eight thousand feet.

In my opinion, there are too many sub-regions exist in the Caribbean.

There is the English speaking Caribbean, which comprised of Guyana, Trinidad and Tobago, Grenada, St Vincent and the Grenadines, St Lucia, Dominica, Montserrat, Antigua and Barbuda, St Kitts and Nevis, Jamaica, Turks and Caicos, Anguilla, Cayman Islands, US and British Virgin Islands, Barbados and the Bahamas. Some of these islands have formed the Organization for Eastern Caribbean States. Belize is also called an English speaking Caribbean nation.

The French West Indies include Martinique, Haiti, Guadeloupe, St Bath and Saint Martin. All of these islands are Departments of France.

The Dutch Caribbean or Netherland Antilles are the ABC islands – Aruba, Bonaire and Curacao. Other islands include Saba and St Maarten. Sometimes, Suriname is deemed a Dutch Caribbean country.

Spanish speaking Caribbean are those islands that speak Spanish – Puerto Rico, the Dominican Republic and Cuba.

There are also more developed countries, or Greater Antilles. These nations are the bigger islands amongst the Eastern Caribbean and are more developed; Jamaica, Trinidad and Tobago and Barbados that is moderately developed but small in land area – a mere one hundred and sixty six square miles island. These islands have sizeable population.

In fact, the lesser develop countries, or Lesser Antilles exist. These countries are deemed less developed and are smaller in land area compared to Jamaica and Trinidad and Tobago. Interestingly, these are the nations that formed the Organization for Eastern Caribbean States – Grenada, St Vincent and the Grenadines, St Lucia, Dominica, Montserrat, Antigua and Barbuda, St Kitts and Nevis and Anguilla.

There are the overseas territories and Departments. These countries are dependent on European countries and their operations are sanctioned by the head of states in Europe.

The Windward Islands are four of the English speaking nations. They comprised of Dominica, St Lucia, St Vincent and the Grenadines and Grenada. They formed the Windward Islands Banana Association; an association to the Guest Industry in England. These Countries also formed the Windward Island Cricket team. The Windward Islands are located in the southern Caribbean with Martinique situated half way between Dominica and St Lucia.

Finally, there are the Leeward Islands. This sub-region is composed of Antigua and Barbuda, St Kitts and Nevis, Montserrat and Anguilla. These islands are also English speaking and are located in the northern part of the region. They formed the Leeward Islands cricket team.

This in itself has, over many decades, sparked many controversy and disputes between the nations. Some nation identified themselves as French Caribbean and some Spanish speaking; therefore, they are identified with a particular group instead of a united Caribbean.

A huge number of people see themselves as countries from more developed countries, who believe that that they have higher status in life than the people from the lesser developed countries. A phrase used by people from the more developed countries is, "Your country is small and ghetto."

The dependent territories see themselves as having greater financial mobility than the independent sovereign countries. Immigrants to these islands are normally deemed as foreigners.

Similar problems exist in the United States. America is comprised of too many sub-regions – the Midwest, the east coast, the west coast, and northern and southern states.

Many citizens from the northern states see people from the states as more racial and promoted slavery within the states. Northerners often see southerners as people who speak with different accents.

East coast rivals against west coast. One of the reasons for the deaths of the Notorious B.I.G and Tupac is consequent to this identity group. This was evident in the rappers behavior about their hate for one another.

We should take a lesson from the Europeans; the formed and the European Union and that's how they identified themselves, instead of East, north, south and west Europe.

It seemed as though the Caribbean has good intention, however, for some apparent reason the regions has failed to fully integrate. In 1958, the Caribbean colonies of Britain formed a regional alliance in an effort to establish a united political front, which would allow the dependent territories to gain their independence from Britain as a single state.

This regional movement only lasted for about four years – due to political conflicts amongst the nations.

The Caribbean has the obligation to assess its situation and defines the problems in the political arena and find solutions to fix these graved issues.

Today, the Caribbean is developing at a very slow rate, because of its unstable political and economical environments. Some cities have developed with Western features, while some islands still have the touch of European civilization. Gradually, most of our societies are changing and adapting to western ideologies - specifically the North American way of life.

With the introduction of cable television in the region, there should be no doubt that our way of life have started to take shape like that of the United

States; hence, our identity is West Indians are slowly diminishing.

Let me just mention that most of the Caribbean nations are experiencing brain drain - loosing educated people to International countries and sometimes within the region its self, which is not too disadvantageous for us if we regionalized our efforts.

Some educated people leave the region for United States of America, Canada and England to take up domestic jobs. Some of them are even living illegally in these international nations. This is consequent to the weakening economies of our nations.

The societies in the Caribbean are different from the other societies located in the Western Hemisphere relative to culture, size and mobility. Small patches of regionalism exist within the region such as the attempt by the English Speaking Caribbean to regionalize the Caribbean through the Caribbean Community and the Caribbean Common Market.

For me there is no real sense of integration within the region other than the West Indies cricket team and the West Indies Cricket Association.

All that is in the air is an environment filled with many talks and no actions.

Too many nations around us are lacking the interest we need to move forward and too many times nations remove themselves from the equation when problem arise; therefore, the effort to carry on is compromised.

Trends indicate that there is a reduction of international supports to the region. Haiti that is bombarded by high volumes crimes, political and economic instability had been ignored until recently the United Nations decided to extend a helping hand.

The United States effects on regionalism in the Caribbean have created lasting impacts.

Faculties, strategies and systems, which were in place to assist the Caribbean in reducing drug trafficking has been pulled back by the United States government under the George W. Bush presidency.

Also, the United States closed its medical institution in St Vincent and the Grenadines for the same reason that St Vincent and the Grenadines association with Socialist states have created some aggravation within the United States government – declaring that the state was going in the wrong direction, therefore, the United States removed its interest in that part of the region.

The United States government under Bill Clinton was against the Lome Convention; an institution which allows banana exporters from the Caribbean to enter cheaply their products into the European Union. Subsequently, the Europeans had to discontinue these benefits these Caribbean Islands enjoyed. The United States accomplished this by imposing tariffs on European goods.

Ideally, the United States has caused hundreds of farmers to experience fallen profit while expenditure increases; hence, the reason for the cultivation of illegal drugs amongst many farmers.

Not forgetting that the Europeans have had economic impact on regionalism in the Caribbean. Many Caribbean nations have extended tax break for Unites States companies operating in the region, but the Europeans have made this a problems and described the Caribbean as tax havens.

As a result of this, there were tight legislation enacted to deal with money laundering and conditions in which an international company could operate out of these islands.

Countries like the United States, Canada, England the European Union do not have interest in the Caribbean, therefore, they would lose focus. The Caribbean must survive on its own, since these countries have backed off. In light of this, I believe that this is the time to start the integration process.

When the world confronts us they must do so to a collective body. I am aware that when the United States pressured the Europeans to disconnect the Lome Convention that each island's leader was contacted separately, therefore, the pressure would be enormous. It would be different if they each nation as a unit.

However, there is new international relation between countries like Taiwan, Iran, and Venezuela developed amongst Caribbean Islands. These countries are playing the roles that the United States and Britain are obliged to carry out.

Assistance is rendered in the medical field by these countries where they provide medical facilities and invested in many other projects especially in the agriculture, light manufacturing and business sectors.

Countries like the Turks and Caicos Islands and the Bahamas that are closer to the United States are more prone to the American ways of life.

They also travel very often to different parts of the United States.

The islands often boast about having one identity, but when this vision is being implemented its people revolt.

It is my recommendation again for the region to seek guidance from the European Union that has successfully integrated.

The Caribbean is a nice little place where everyone can live in harmony.

~ PART 2 ~

Sports

It has been one hundred years since the West Indies cricket team were established. The West Indies as colloquially termed have representatives from about twelve different islands in the Caribbean. For decades the team mainly selected players from Trinidad and Tobago, Barbados, Jamaica, Guyana and the Leeward Islands – Antigua and Barbuda, St Kitts and Nevis and Anguilla, a small British dependent Island in the northern Caribbean. Although, for many years the West Indies had no representatives from the Windward Islands –Dominica, St Lucia, St Vincent and the Grenadines and Grenada, these nations had always gave the West Indies their full support and followed the team where ever they played.

I grew up listening to the West Indies played cricket throughout the world including the Caribbean. In the Windward Islands we did not have the leisure of seeing the West Indies perform, as the team played all their matches in Trinidad and Tobago, Barbados, Antigua and Barbuda, Guyana and Jamaica. However, we as a nation we never felt left out as this was what a true Caribbean brand was all about.

In St Vincent and the Grenadines, although there were no Vincentians on the team, we still referred to the West Indies Players as *our boys*.

We grew up hearing that the Caribbean was one nation and that what we'd believed in all these years.

The fact remained that the West Indies cricket team was a winner at the time, we'd be foolish if we did not associate ourselves with that "Winning team."

Conversely, in the latter part of the collapse of the West Indies cricket team players from the Windward Islands began to make their debut on the international scene. In my opinion, and maybe the assertion of many Vincentian, or for that matter Windward Islanders, their players were not treated the same as those from the popular islands. Therefore, only a few players had made it thus far – Cameron Cuffy, Ian Allen, Junior Murray, Rawl Lewis, Deighton Butler, Dave Smith, and Nixon McLean who I am proud to mention, since we competed against each other in the local inter-secondary school tournament in St Vincent and the Grenadines.

Other Windward Islanders – Rawl Lewis and Junior Murray from Grenada have also debut on the international scene for the West Indies. A few other Windward Islanders from St Lucia and Dominica had also made their debuts.

Is this a fact? Well one has to evaluate this phenomenon for themselves, or maybe other West Indians will see it differently if they especially are not from St Vincent and the Grenadines or other parts of the Windward Islands. The evidence showed that most of the Windward Islands players place on the team was short lived.

Moreover, trends show that the Windward islanders only made the team when one of the popular' islands players is bombarded by injuries; hence, a player form the Windward Islands is called to make his debut.

This was foil play on part of the Windward islander - a debut that promotes failure to the player as evidence to the rest of the Caribbean Community that Windward Islanders do not have the necessary skills and ability to play at that level.

Many West Indians asked why players from the Windward Islands cricket team do not stay for any long period of time with the West Indies cricket team.

This question arises as a consequence to the Windward Islands having the worse regional records.

Some argued that the Windward Islands are seen as small island nations and that the West Indies selectors rather play cricketers from the larger islands. But ask yourself if this is particularly true? I don't think so! Dominica, St Lucia, Grenada and St Vincent and the Grenadines are bigger islands than Antigua, St Kitts and Nevis, Montserrat, Anguilla, and even Barbados that has its own team and is only bigger than St Vincent and the Grenadines and Grenada in the Windward Islands.

Particularly, Barbados has only become popular because of its stable economy, which arises out of the country's industrial environment.

Hitherto, Antigua and Barbuda are also two tiny islands, but I believe that its popularity ignited from the legacy that Sir Vivian Richards had left behind.

Other persons especially those from the larger territories – Jamaica, Trinidad and Tobago, Barbados and Guyana argued that the Windward Islands cricket team is the weakest team amongst the Caribbean nations. So true, but is this the real reason? I don't think so.

To argue this point, Clayton Lambert the Guyanese open batsman made the West Indies team on one of the West Indies tour to England. At the time Dawnley Joseph the open batsman from the Windward Islands was performing well. In spite of this, Clayton Lambert were selected on the team ahead of Dawnley Joseph. In England, Clayton Lambert failed miserably.

How can we explain this?

The point that I am making here is that the players from the popular islands are given first preferences, regardless their regional performances.

A similar action by the West Indies selectors occurred on an Australian tour when Philo Wallace, an opening batsman from Barbados was selected for the

West Indies team. He failed to perform to West Indies standard.

There was much talk in St Vincent and the Grenadines and I assume throughout the Windward Islands about this pick.

The real truth for the lack of exposure on the West Indies cricket team for Windward Islanders was that all of the selectors were from the more recognized countries at the time, therefore, the Windward Islanders had limited or no chance in making the team.

Is this a fear conclusion? Yes I would say, but nevertheless as people from the Windward Islander we have always been step by step behind the West Indies cricket team.

At least this occurred during my time of listening and following cricket.

Whenever cricket was played whether at home or somewhere around the world it would create oneness in the region. Everyone sat carefully behind their television screen. Sometimes, staying up all night watching the West Indies dismantling other teams. Those of us who had to work would carry our radio and followed the game along the way.

I know people from St Vincent and the Grenadines who buy small exercise books and recorded every score the commentators revealed.

One without lost, five without last, nine without lost, nine for one wicket, and so on.

Subsequently, the West Indies was one of the strongest, if not the strongest team for more than three decades. Back then, the team clearly defined the word integration amongst Caribbean nations. In fact, a person who never held a dictionary could assess the environment in the Caribbean during the team's performance and know what integration is all about. In the true sense, the West Indies could not survive that long if they had individual teams; therefore, we must come together to make the perfect team.

I must highlight though, that a few international matches were played at Arnos Vale playing field in St Vincent and the Grenadines. Some of these one day matches played long before I was born and some a few years ago when West Indies scheduled two consecutive One Day Internationals at that unique location.

In my life time, as other St Vincentians and other Windward Islanders, I have had the opportunity to see the West Indies perform right at home.

As expected many Vincentians turned out to these matches and the feedback from the commentators had indicated that Arnos Vale had become one of the best cricket venues in the Caribbean and the most picturesque grounds in the world with a background view of one of the sister islands of Bequia. I remembered when the commentators announced this fact during a one day game the local crowd went wild.

St Vincent and Grenadines would normally host two consecutive One Day International games at the Arnos Vale playing field; thereafter the host country would lose its two One Day International games to the new venue - a new national stadium, which is built in Grenada.

A lot of Vincentians in particular had angered this decision, but one would argue that this was a well-thought of and valid decision by the West Indies Cricket Board – the WICB. To be fair this was a move, which would benefit Grenada and the board as a whole.

The reason for the new venue was primarily based on the fact that mainland St Vincent had limited hotel accommodations for the players and the visiting team and for the many spectators that followed their teams.

More so, the airport facilities present at the E.T Joshua airport was not accommodating enough for the many regional and international flights, which were intended to fly to the Island. E.T Joshua airport is only four and a half thousand feet long.

Additionally, I believe that the facilities at Arnos vale playing field needed some upgrades.

The big set back here, and I understood why some Vincentians was dissatisfied, is that economically the country was about to lose some of its businesses to Grenada - tourism, recognition and some free marketing.

The Caribbean as a whole has a passion for cricket. Everyone would teach you the game even if they have never picked up a bat, or hold a ball in their hands – everyone in the Caribbean knows and live cricket.

As the boys, as we often referred to them, walked out in their pretty white trousers and shirts, the local West Indian crowd would stand in recognition of the great men of the team. They seemed even more professional when they wear the old English sweater over their uniform.

Our team really defined greatness and everyone would agree. It is a fact that the other world teams had individual players, but doesn't matter how good these players were when they came to the Caribbean, or for that matter played against the West Indies they could not perform.

Graham Gooch of England was a great batman but could not shine against the West Indies; Waqar Younis from Pakistan was one of the fastest bowlers in the World, but he was often *beaten off his line* by our players mostly, Richie Richardson, the great Sir Vivian Richards and the world record holder Brian Lara.

As West Indians we could all say that the West Indies had done us proud. They were so strong that the rest of the world would have to team up against them, a match up in which the rest of the world would still be defeated; the simple fact remained – we were too strong.

In fact, a number of West Indies players were contracted to play county cricket in England and later on in different parts of the world including South Africa and India.

On the contrast the West Indies after the captaincy of Sir Vivian Richards had crumbled along the way. Some teams, which were not recognized, out-performed the West Indies; Sri Lanka, New Zealand, Kenya and Bangladesh – West Indies was losing its winning stream and the Caribbean will also lose its unity.

During this time, there were many disgruntled people. The united environment throughout the Caribbean, which cricket had created was not the same anymore – the defeat of the team was taking that high spirit down with it, one would agree. Many Caribbean people did not associate themselves with the West Indies team once it started to lose to other teams. Everyone was blaming the defeat on individual team player. "It was the selfish opening batman from Trinidad, or the stupid bowler from Jamaica." These were some of the phrases heard around the region.

I remember one night I was listening to a radio call-in program in Barbados during a West Indies tour of Australia, when one caller from Barbados went on the air and purported that the West Indies should come back home in light of their poor performance. It was a team that had Desmond Haynes and Philo Wallace as opening batsmen on a West Indies tour to

Australia – this is all I remembered about the team on that tour.

The stands and the cricket arena were quiet in the Caribbean and West Indies supporters started to get personal with the visiting team, while they defeated West Indies in every game they played.

Again, once England tour of the West Indies resulted in chaos when they were defeating the West Indies at Kensington Oval in Barbados and the spectators threw bottles on the grounds. Courtney Walsh the lanky Jamaican swing bowler had to calm the crowd. The West Indies could not get a grip on their winnings again, therefore, the Barbadians and other West Indians who were following the team turned to throwing bottles and other objects on the field - stopping play time for a few minutes.

This was one thing that West Indians could not live with. They were accustoming winning every game and dismantled every team that spins the toss against them.

Losing was a new way of life for us - we could not face life on the other side and we could not adapt to this environment.

After closely scrutinizing the era in which the West Indies were losing to the world, it is not that our boys didn't have what it takes to play cricket any more, or lack of integration of the Caribbean Islands, but it is consequent to a number of factors:

First, the West Indies Cricket Board did not have enough money to sustain the team. In this capacity, it is my opinion. Meanwhile, countries like Australia and England were investing money into the sport; creating a school where their players play cricket for a living. The West Indies Cricket Board, was in no way, equipped to do this; therefore, Australian players would out-perform the West Indies and other cricketing nations around the world.

The Australians did not impact the game or out-performed the West Indies because of talent amongst the players, but their success came as a result of vision and strategy.

The West Indies Cricket Board could not see this far, neither do they have enough resources to adapt the Australian strategy.

Moreover, the West Indies were relying on individual talents, such as Brian Lara while Australia produced a team - big difference.

This is evident in Brian Lara's second world record of scoring the most runs – it occurred when the West Indies were losing to every team.

Once Brian Lara was out of the game, the other team could count them all out.

West Indians became so frustrated that they turned some of their frustration on Brian Lara. Although, Brian Lara is not one of my favorites, for some unwelcome comments toward St Vincentians, he was being targeted for some apparent reasons.

He was accused for match fixing and selling out the game sometimes.

There is no evidence that he did, therefore, the Caribbean Community was wrong about the way he was targeted and demised. After all he is the world's record holder.

Second, the 1994 World Cup Soccer in Atlanta, United States, had changed the environment in St Vincent and the Grenadines. I also believe that these soccer games had impacted the entire Caribbean. In St Vincent and the Grenadines everyone stopped playing cricket and everywhere was a soccer match, whether it is between two people or a full team; in the road or on the field - World Cup Soccer had come closer to home.

There were some big names in the tournament, particular Diego Maradona of Argentina, who topped the list of best players in the world at the time. Andres Escobar of Columbia was also a star player of the games. Roberto Baggio of Italy was amongst the finest players who were expected to play well in that tournament. These big names have sparked a new beginning in the minds and careers of the young sport fanatics in the region.

Third, as proclaimed on the streets throughout the Caribbean from both sides, there was some cynicism about the notion of "Small island people," meaning islands in the Caribbean with a smaller area size and population. This is how the larger islands like Jamaican and Trinidad and Tobago would address someone from smaller islands, such as St Lucia or Grenada; giving the impression that we are small and not good enough to be placed on the West Indies cricket team.

This was not so much the case of the Trinidadians.

But how do we explain the Antiguans, Anguillians and the Kittitians who played for the team. I figured that players like Vivian Richards, Richie Richardson and Any Roberts had paved the way for them.

Nevertheless, I believe that there were players from the Windward Islands who could have performed if given the chance. Players such as, John Eugene of St Lucia; Roy Marshalls of Dominica; Casper Davis and Dawnley Joseph of St Vincent and the Grenadines to name a few, had performed well for the Windward Island Cricket team for many years, and they were not even given a trial.

Fourth, I have concluded that the International Cricket Council had over the years changes many rules of the game. In my honest opinion, these rules were changed in favor of the other teams. The West Indies bowlers especially had to change the way they bowl – *as more than one bouncer in an over could result in disciplinary actions.*

Last, the fact that cricket at the time had no money. When you consider the amount of money a soccer player made, or a basketball player, salaries paid to cricketers were in no way close to those salaries paid to athletes in the other sports; hence the reason for players to focus more on sports, which were attractive relative to paid salaries.

How can we blame young West Indians for their change of mind?

For the same reason other athletes are leaning to the more attractive salaries.

In addition to this, the salaries that each of these player received were far beyond what the entire West Indies cricket team were receiving.

In an effort to revived our cricket team we must invest some money into the sport and make it attractive for people who have the skills, or even want to develop their skills. I also believe that the West Indies Cricket Board must have some strong hold in the International Cricket Council decision making process and not just taking orders. Foremost, there is the need to pick a fear team from all the Islands if the right players are available; however, if a team cannot be represented in the West Indies team at any given time we must understand that - It worked that way before and it could still happen. But most importantly, we must integrate, not only through cricket but in other aspects of the region. Our cricket could rejuvenate and rise to be the best again - we have integrated the Caribbean through cricket, therefore, let us build on our past success and look at other factors of integration.

We must also continue the regional competition to derive the best players to represent us. For me, it does not matter if all the players come from Guyana, Trinidad and Tobago, Leeward Islands, Barbados, or Jamaica, the fact is we have selected our best team that would come together to conquer the world.

It is obvious that many people would see themselves as individual islands; this is not surprising as it is natural for people to think that way. My suggestion is that we stop thinking individualism and think collectivism – thinking collective is going to take us a long way. With the limited and scarce resources, which are available to us we are not able to stand individually – at least not through sports.

If we are not sure about how to conquer the world as a single Caribbean, Let's follow-suit the United States of America. Some may argue that the United States are one country, but it boils down to the same thing – cooperation toward a single goal.

If one go back in time when the United States were individual countries with imaginary borders, one would find out that these countries had seen it fit to amalgamate in an effort to be more efficient and productive. Today people in America still label themselves as Californians, Texans, New Yorkers, from the south or north, from the east or west or even Mideast sometimes, but when it comes to confronting the rest of the world they often see themselves as Americans. One would also agree that these countries could have stayed apart. It is evident that this strategy had worked well for the United States of America.

Why can't the Caribbean adopt this strategy and move ahead? For me I will always be a St Vincentian and you and you will always be a Trinidadian or Guyanese or a Bahamian, but when it comes to competing, we must see ourselves as one – West Indians.

I could say the same about Canada and its thirteen Proveniences. I have heard Canadians introduced themselves as Nova Scotians, Québécois, French Canadian, *Newfies*, and even *Maritimers*. However, when it involves the world outside, they called themselves Canadians.

These provinces have their own sporting activities, but they would never face the world as individual provinces, but as team Canada. Canada's hockey team is comprised of players from across Canada; Nova Scotia, Ontario and British Columbia.

The Caribbean does attend these sports meets, but as team St Vincent and the Grenadines, team Trinidad and Tobago, team or Jamaica and the like, there is no other single Caribbean team other than the West Indies Cricket team.

The Caribbean are many islands with their own government, which I understand, all we need to do is to create a Caribbean Council or commission to oversee all the operations within the region.

To create a recognized Caribbean brand the other sports played within the region must also be integrated into one. The Caribbean mostly participate in Netball, Soccer, table and lawn tennis, basketball, which is on the rise; and athletics, which is more popular in Jamaica, Cuba, the Bahamas, Trinidad and Tobago, and gradually gaining grounds in Barbados.

I believe that the other sports should be integrated also. Instead of having a Trinidadian soccer team or a Jamaican soccer team, there should be a Caribbean team. I am not purporting this idea, because Jamaica and Trinidad and Tobago have gone to two world cup games, but I am sure that their result would have been better if there was a Caribbean team at those world cup games. As the old saying, "Unity is strength."

There are out-standing performers in the rest of the Caribbean that can assist in building a team, which could put up resistance amongst the other world teams. Martinique had always performed well in the Confederation of North, Central America and the Caribbean Association Football - CONCACAF. St Vincent and the Grenadines that has placed second in the championship in 1996 and had played in the world cup qualifying round against Mexico, Honduras and Costa Rica. Barbados and Surinam also have talented players; not withholding the Republic of Haiti that had the record for being the first Caribbean country to enter the world cup. Again if Haiti had merge into a Caribbean team I believe that results would be much better.

This coupled with the many talents, which exist in Trinidad and Tobago and Jamaica.

In the meantime Cuba and Guyana are becoming a team to be reckoned with.

Our countries, as single nations, do not possess enough resources to stand on their own against the world where people play football for a living - they get paid for playing soccer. As a young man growing up in the Caribbean, we play soccer in season for the love of the game.

Furthermore, when our players are at work hustling for a living to provide for their families, players from Mexico, United States, England or Asia, are on the field practicing or playing club soccer all year round, and making millions of dollars.

In this capacity, I am in favor of employing investors to come into the Caribbean and develop sports. Parks throughout the islands could be developed and have club soccer similar to those played in England and other parts of Europe and now the United States of America. Growing up in Georgetown, I remember the thousands of people who would swamp the park in Chili Village to watch their favorite teams. I believe this project could be a success. Thus, this could create more demand for air, land and sea transport in the region and, therefore, provide jobs for athlete and other citizens alike.

To attract investments into this there is a need to bring in international players. This strategy is also useful in developing regional players – having the opportunity to compete against players who possess different styles of the game. This will attract other investors into the project also.

Ideally, our leaders need to create a business plan and sell it to the potential investors around the world.

Investors to target are found in England and Europe, the United States and Canada.

The region, on its own cannot even finance a Caribbean tournament nor do we have enough resources – especially players to sustain a single championship. We must fight the giants and among them are the United States, Canada, Mexico, Honduras and Costa Rica. Why not host a regional tournament, pick a regional team and play against the United States, Canada, Mexico, Honduras, Costa Rica and other countries? This is the direction we should take.

These giants are part of our zone and we must defeat them in an effort to enter the world cup.

I realized that countries like Jamaica and Trinidad and Tobago may decline this strategy for the sole reason that they have defeated the odds and made their way to the world – but look at their results thereafter.

Trinidad front runners Dwight York and Russell Latapy alone cannot sustain the Soca Warriors.

Taking everything into consideration, we cannot enter an individual team to the world cup and expect results.

At least I could speak about Jamaica and Trinidad and Tobago. However, I do not have much information about Haiti's world cup history as it was the same year I was born - 1974.

But the one thing I could point out is that Haiti did not make it past the first round. Actually, they failed to win a single game in their zone, which comprised Poland, Italy and Argentina. In fact, Poland place second in that year and scored seven goals to one when they played Haiti.

Jamaica, when they entered the world cup was fully supported by the Caribbean; at least I could vow for St Vincent and the Grenadines that followed and supported the reggae boys all the way. The team only defeated Japan and never past the first round. From my prospective, Jamaica was only there to create awareness for Jamaica and not really to win – considering teams such as Brazil, Italy, Germany to name a few of the world soccer giants.

All you could hear in the street, bars and everywhere you go was Jamaica and the reggae boys; where does the Caribbean comes in? This was supposed to be a Caribbean effort. Then comes the nasty comments about the other parts of the Caribbean that had not made it to the world cup – they see us as "Small Island people," who cannot make a name for ourselves. It was not supposed to be this way – it was supposed to be a, "Caribbean thing."

Trinidad and Tobago was the most recent after missing there chance a few years earlier, even before Jamaica was qualified for the world cup. Trinidad and Tobago had played against the United States of America in the finals of the World cup qualifying round. Again St Vincent and the Grenadines and the rest of the Caribbean were supporting the neighboring team – the Soca Warriors. At the High school I attended, the headmaster then gave the student leisure to watch the match as we recognized this game to be history making for the Caribbean. Despite this, the Caribbean still does not have a regional team. I often asked myself, why? The Soca Warriors lost the game, which created a tense, heartbroken and painful environment amongst nations of the region. This was an opportunity the Caribbean could not afford to lose. Although, it was Trinidad and Tobago making a way for them on the international soccer arena, the Caribbean – with its perceived oneness – was looking forward to support their very own; the twin islands republic.

The twin republic later made it to the world cup, which they well deserved and yet did not make it past the first round; this was in an effort to introduce the *"Trini*-brand."

But I do not blame the Trinidadians. I figured if St Vincent and the Grenadines had made it to the world cup games back in the early 1990's that the *Vincy* Heats would be creating awareness for St Vincent and the Grenadines, and not a Caribbean effort.

Hence, the individual efforts.

To be truthful I had never heard the Trinidadians with any sort of arrogance. I was left with the impression that they are really Caribbean oriented and that they are not responsible for sending their own team to the world cup – let's blame the heads of government in the Caribbean for their lack of vision and oneness.

The Caribbean has not made any significant progress in the sports of soccer; however, there are a few individual players who have made it on the international scene in Europe and North America

– Russell Latapy and Dwight York from Trinidad and Tobago to name a few from the best.

Another sport, which and few countries in the region had excel is netball, a culturally played sports like cricket and soccer. Ideally, a number of countries in the Caribbean have made their marks in this unique sport. Trinidad and Tobago Soca Warriors, St Vincent and the Grenadines *Vincy* Heats and Jamaica Sunshine Girls, and the Barbadian team have shared many regional championships. Jamaica and Trinidad and Tobago have placed in the world tournament behind the well-known Australian and English teams.

If the domineering Sunshine Girls and the spectacular *Soca Girls* could have a place in the world games then having a West Indies Netball team would certainly do wonders. Let's stop representing St Vincent and the Grenadines; stop representing Jamaica; stop representing Trinidad and Tobago; and stop representing Barbados – therefore, we must represent the West Indies.

The region has produced decorated netball players for decades now and I am sure that we could find extra players elsewhere in the Caribbean – let's create the Caribbean brand.

St Vincent and the Grenadines has placed third in the 2008 Caribbean Net Association Jean Pierre Under sixteen tournament and four of the island's player namely Sheldene Joseph, Tonique Bowen, Ruthann Williams and Mary Ann Federick were name among the top players in the tournament – can we build a champion West Indies Netball team? My recommendation is that we should only compete amongst ourselves in an effort to build the regional team that would upset the rest of the world when we put foot on their turf, or whether they come to visit us.

I also dream about netball arenas be built throughout the Caribbean to host champion ship games, where Caribbean players could earn a full time salary playing netball. More so, this should adopt the same idea of creating parks to accommodate soccer championships. We need more tournaments like the "Clash of the Champions," where all the winners from netball clubs in each island would compete against each other at one championship meet in Arnos Vale sporting complex each year. I strongly believe this influenced Allen Standard twenty20 cricket championships in Antigua, Antigua and Barbuda.

Let's turn our focus to basketball; another sport widely played in the Caribbean. I must admit that basketball is not as popular as the other sports relative to players' performance, at the least, this is my opinion. However, we have produced many international basketball players who had either played in the National Basketball Association – NBA, or are presently playing for a team in the European Union, and now the Women National Basketball Association - WNBA.

This is another sport where we can excel globally, because the Caribbean currently has players who are playing worldwide. I could name at least four players from the Caribbean who are currently playing for the NBA; Raja Bells of Phoenix Suns from St Croix; Samuel Dalembert of Philadelphia 76ers from Port-au-Prince, Haiti; Tim Duncan of San Antonio from St Croix; and Adonal Foyle of Orlando Magic from St Vincent and the Grenadines.

Other players who can claim the right as a Caribbean citizen are Trevor Ariza who was born in Miami, Florida to Turks and Caicos Island parents and Dan Gaduric of the Milwaukee Bucks the Dutch player whose mother is from Yugoslavia and his father from St Vincent and the Grenadines.

Throughout the years players from the Caribbean have been making a name for themselves and their country. From Patrick Ewing of Jamaica, Carlos Arroya of Puerto Rico, Francisco Garcia of the Dominican Republic; Ken Charles of Trinidad and Tobago, and Mychal Thompson of the Bahamas – there are many other players from Dominica and the Republic of Cuba.

Don't forget the two ambitious ladies from St Vincent and the Grenadines who have made a name for themselves and their country in the WNBA - Sancho Lyttle and Sophia Young.

My question is why couldn't the region build a team together, considering all the talents we have and use these talents to play against the world?

Why do our players have to travel to places like The United States, Canada and Europe in showcasing their skills on an individual basis? Sometimes the odds are against them considering the enormous talents out there. In light of this, I prefer to see a Caribbean basketball team going up against other nations or even have their own team within the NBA, or WNBA, than sending individuals to represent their home island and themselves.

As it relates to the NBA, or the WNBA I believe that we are still too individualistic. All these players have done is to show up on the radar and make millions, when these recognitions should be implemented to create a Caribbean brand.

Finally, let me discuss athletics in the Caribbean and how it impacts the region. The big names here are Jamaica, Trinidad and Tobago, the Bahamas and Cuba, with some talents in Barbados and Antigua and Barbuda. There are enormous talents in countries such as Haiti, the Dominican Republic and Guyana, but their economic instability would not allow them to even shine at the regional level. My point is, should we have a Caribbean team we would have enough resources to build these talents we have unattended.

Individual nations within the region have made it on the world stage. I mostly recognized Ato Boldon, the "Bombastic" Trinidadian one hundred meter sprinter. He got this "bombastic" name because of the way he walked to the line prior to the pulling of the trigger on the track. It is the way the athlete boost themselves before the race starts, I must say.

In my view, Boldon paved the way for many Caribbean athletes on the track, including the world record holder Usain Bolt. Boldon had won many championships throughout the Caribbean and across the world including a silver medal in the 2000 Olympic Games – one hundred meters, gold medal at the 1997 world championships in Athens – two hundred meters, gold medal at the 2003 Pan American Games in Santo Domingo – four by one hundred meters and gold medal in the 1992 World Junior Championships in Seoul – one and two hundred meters, amongst other championship titles. As usual the Caribbean were behind the twin island Republic of Trinidad and Tobago.

The Bahamians and the Cubans would do well meanwhile, and the Jamaicans who produce two of the world fastest men ever – Asafa Powel who had broke the record on several occasions and now the speedster Usain Bolt who out-performed everyone who ran close him in the 2008 Beijing Olympic Games. This youngster ran so fast and with his last name was given the nick name, "Lightning bolt."

During the Beijing Olympic Games the entire Caribbean were supporting the Jamaicans; they were happy to see, for the first time, a countryman had took over the track other than the United States at such a high level. More so, the Island of Jamaica is seen as a small poor crime-stricken island in the West

Indies. Everyone was glad to see the change, even the Turks and Caicos who thought they were being represented by the high performance of the Jamaicans until some Jamaicans implied that the Caribbean was nothing without Jamaica. This did not resonate well amongst other Caribbean nationalities; then comes the disputes amongst Jamaicans and other Caribbean nations. Some Jamaican nationals also implied that the talents, which were being displayed at the games, could not be found elsewhere in the Caribbean, Guyanese, Vincentians, St Lucians, Turks Islanders, and others were furious. Suddenly, the support went dimmed and the Jamaicans were left to stand – other parts of the Caribbean would turn their backs on them for such arrogance.

This is evident that we are too individualistic. Should we blame the Jamaicans for their behaviors? Some had purported that this is part of their culture, but I begged to differ. If our heads of government do not put things in place to regionalized the region then everyone is right to see themselves as individual nations striving on their own accord. If nothing is in place through a federation then we cannot assume that we are many nations under one roof. I believe in the proverb, "Action speaks louder than words."

With such strong and offensive comments, the Caribbean cannot strife as one. I would like to see a Caribbean athletic team. As far as my mind could take me back, islands like St Vincent and the Grenadines, Anguilla, St Lucia, Grenada and many other Caribbean Islands have yet to win a medal at the Olympic Games, therefore, why send these representatives.

The region should set a standard from the Commonwealth Games, or the Caribbean Free Trade Association Games – CARIFTA, and those who cannot make that standard should not be allowed to take part in any event. There are talents out there that we have to match and sending a team of men for the sake of sending is not enough and wise.

Sending a team to the Olympic or any athletic meets is, in my opinion, a waste of resources, which could have been used to enhance and sustain regional athletes. Some countries send two and three athletes to some games, hoping that they will work magic and out-perform the bigger talents. Again let's build a Caribbean brand. Even if the team only comprise of Bahamians, Jamaicans, Trinidadian and Cubans, they are representing the Caribbean and not individual countries.

For the bigger countries they possess more talents, because of their large population - the bigger the demographics, the more talents is exist.

Looking at the trends surround St Lucia, Anguilla, Grenada and St Vincent and the Grenadines, If each island spent one hundred thousand dollars to prepared athletes who would not even place at the games, why not take that money to help power up the "Caribbean team" and reap the benefits – to sustain the Caribbean brand.

Not surprising that some people may argue that the Europeans had joined together and yet they have individual teams. This is a fact, but the truth is that Europe has so many talents and resources that they have to carry their own teams. Countries like England, Italy and Germany can send five soccer teams to the world cup and still perform. These countries have millions and millions of people and talents to their exposure. If there should be a European soccer team or basketball ball team, there would be too many talents sitting on the bench waiting for their turn, which might never come. On the contrast, the Caribbean does not have this enormous talent and resources at their exposure.

If you remove, Haiti, the Dominican Republic and Cuba that have almost thirty five million people the rest of the Caribbean is left with just a mere fraction of this amount. Only Jamaica, Trinidad and Tobago and Puerto Rico have a relatively large population, total of almost ten million. The thing to remember is that these are the countries, which are economically unstable except for Puerto Rico that is part of the United States.

Smaller islands in the Eastern Caribbean are hardly populated expect for Barbados and the Bahamas that have almost four hundred thousand people; Martinique with just over four hundred thousand; and Guadeloupe and Guyana that barely past six hundred thousand people.

Countries in the Eastern Caribbean, the Bahamas, Turks and Caicos Islands and Guyana do not even have half of the population of Jamaica.

This is why we need to amalgamate and share our vision and other resources.

I must highlight that the Bahamas are the only independent state that I doing well economically. The Eastern Caribbean is average and other British and American dependent countries in the Caribbean have well sustained economies. My point is that it is hard for these countries sustain a competitive sporting environment and the fact that there are minimal talents within these territories.

Therefore, the bigger countries have more talents and the smaller islands have more monetary resources available to them, hence, my quest is to bring all the money and talents together and put them to one use.

In this sense, a bigger nation suggests that there are more talents to choose from, hence, a stronger team. Many countries around the world have millions of people, in addition to a number of available resources and institutions; therefore, it is difficult to compete against them.

The same reason that small nations will always be lagging behind.

Let's used our resources effectively and stop competing amongst ourselves.

Ideally, sports tourism will eventually escalate within the region if we integrate all aspects of sports. This would create awareness for the entire region and could bring about enormous improvement in the economy because sports brings money; the many spectators who will be coming in support of their home teams. Look at the impact the Cricket World Cup had on the region it sold thousands of tickets and entice worldwide media coverage. It was a time when many airlines including our own LIAT became busy, taking it to the skies, hotels were sold out and vendors ran out of items to sell.

These monies can be spent to improve our facilities and technology to the standard exists in the rest of the world. Sport tourism also bring talents to the Caribbean; talents, which could be adapted and learnt, hence, enhancing the quality of the players.

Meeting the world as individual teams cannot be maintained. If so, we are doing it to compete among ourselves, to market our self as individual islands. We must not tell the world that Trinidad and Tobago has the best cricket team; or St Vincent and the Grenadines has the best netball team; or the best basketball team is in the Bahamas; or the most efficient soccer team is in Martinique; or the best-performed athletes come from Jamaica. Rather we must indicate that the best sporting team, whether it may be cricket, basketball, soccer or netball, is from the Caribbean.

This is what defines regionalism.

From a regional prospective, this would be the correct thing to do.

We have the right idea when we introduced the West Indies to the world. Disappointedly, this is where the integration process stopped. For many decades, the West Indies have been on top of their game and brought us together, thereby creating a solid West Indian brand. However, with the losing trends associated with the West Indies we have lost the name and our togetherness. It is time to refocus and build on what our proud players had started many years ago; let revive the spirit of cricket and one nation phenomenon.

If possible we should develop a Caribbean baseball team. The Dominican Republic, Puerto Rico and Cuba have produced great players. These two countries could represent the entire Caribbean, instead on fighting for a place in the spotlight of their own; they might not make it very far despite the many talents there. Without resources especially finance, one cannot sustain oneself. Who cares if the players are primarily Cubans and Dominicans, after all, they are representing all of us. Let's use our competitive advantages to get the job done.

No question why some European countries are so wealthy and powerful in the sports they played; whatever resources they did not possess they search for talents around the world to ascertain those resources they lack. In the Caribbean we have a variety of resources, which we can use, thus, it can only be effective if we put all of these resources together as one.

Many of our talents are leaving home for millions of dollars aboard. This is a perfect plan if we are just looking out for ourselves. What happened to the love ones we left behind?

We should go in a direction that will keep our resources at home, which would allow others to showcase and build their talents, thereby, earning a decent salary while still at home.

Moreover, some of our citizens do have the opportunity to participate in other sports, which are not played at a competitive level in the Caribbean. It is imperative that these sports - golf, swimming, surfing, football and cycling amongst other sporting activities are develop; making us more competitive to the world around us.

To share some light on this, Trinidad and Tobago is big in boat racing - the great race as the *Trinis* refer to it. This sporting activity captures people's attention and the media form around the globe.

Barbados is also known for it Sunday evening races at the Garrison. This sport is on the rise and the *Bajans* have been the highlights in some world horse racing events.

St Vincent and the Grenadines and other Caribbean islands rugby are becoming a popular sport and had gained some attention. The good things here is that the countries are making an effort to maintain this sport - hence, the West Indies Rugby Union.

There are many more sports, which we could develop amongst Caribbean Islands. In this capacity, the region should be able to excel in these sports, which includes swimming, cycling, golfing, parasailing, sailing and surfing, since we have the ideal environment in which to perform.

This is where it is important to have a sustain economy to finance these other sports.

I do not expect the Caribbean to invest in sports, such as hockey and skiing, as we do not have that ideal environment to even attempt to pursue these sports.

I liked the warm, trustful and harmonious environment, which the success of cricket in the region had created. I believe that integrating the other sports played in the region and develop a wider variety of sports represented worldwide by a regional team would certainly bring back that environment, which we as West Indians are accustomed to.

It works for cricket and, therefore, I believe it can work for the other sports.

To do this, we must gather enough resources especially finance and employ the various experts to develop these sports across the region.

Let us look for our talents and carry it to the world, not as individuals but as one where it is possible that we can prosper.

I am aware that results would not come immediately, but it will, and only if we come together as one.

The ball is in our courts, so let's make it happen.

Our work has just begun.

~ **PART 3** ~

Tourism

Each year millions of tourist swamped the lovely shores of the Caribbean; paradise as they called the region, to experience the white sandy beaches and crystal clear blue waters, the culture and the natural environment of the islands.

Some of the most popular islands are the Bahamas, Jamaica, Barbados, Cayman Island and the Virgin Islands, the ABC islands – Aruba, Bonaire and Curacao, and St Lucia, in its own rights is becoming a power house in the Caribbean, relative to its annual total visitors. These islands except for St Lucia are attracting more than one million visitors per year.

In recent years Antigua and Barbuda have been gaining some attention from the world; not because of its magnificent three hundred and sixty five beaches, but the fact that some illegal activities on the twin islands state; therefore, gaining some world-wide scrutiny.

Although Trinidad and Tobago does not boast many attractive white sand beaches it have managed to create an environment, which have attracted an enormous amount of tourist to its shores.

These countries are way ahead of the other islands – Grenada, St Vincent and the Grenadines and Dominica, because of their early development; hence, the reason for these countries being called the more developed countries - the MDC's.

Cuba, Haiti, the Dominican Republic could not go unnoticed considering the sizes of those countries – bigger according to Caribbean standard. Also the political arena in Cuba and Haiti has placed them on the top of the Caribbean chart, although these islands have many enticing white sand beaches and nature trails to their exposure.

Four million people visit the Dominican Republic each year; making it one of the most visited destinations in the Caribbean.

Meanwhile other countries in the region, such as St Vincent and the Grenadines and Grenada are trailing behind the top tourists destinations in the Caribbean. St Vincent and the Grenadines have enormous potentials, but yet to fulfill those demands which tourists are looking for. That country has experienced total annual visitors of more than one hundred thousand at the beginning of the last decade to almost five hundred thousand at the end of the decade.

It's making a name for itself, but not successful enough to get close to the other islands or out-performed them.

The problem, which exists in St Vincent and the Grenadines in particular, and for the other islands that are lagging behind, is the lack of available infrastructure. The biggest threats to the country's progress are its lack of airport facilities, which is needed to accommodate large cargo and commercial jet liners, minimal hotel accommodations and mediocre medical services.

To date Amerijet, a 737 cargo commercial jet is the only cargo plane, which flies into ET Joshua four thousand airport runways. However, other small cargo carriers serve the islands - DHL and FedEx in particular.

Any bigger jet liners must first land on Barbados' Grantley Adams, St Lucia's Hewanorra, or Trinidad Piarco International Airports then divert to St Vincent and the Grenadines on a smaller carrier.

Hitherto, Vincentians normally has to travel to nearby countries for medical attention. Not that St Vincent and the Grenadines does not have good doctors, but the mere fact that we don't have the facilities situated at the Hospitals and medical centers there.

Recently, American Eagle Dash 8 propelled planes with service out of Puerto Rico twice per day with non-stop service to E.T. Joshua airport has terminated its services for reasons pertaining to the safety of E.T. Joshua Airport on mainland St Vincent.

Thereafter, American eagle has begun servicing the tiny Grenadine Island of Canouan.

This set back has created enormous economic losses for the country and difficult times for the many Vincentians, Americans and Puerto Ricans who travel between those three states.

Because if this setback, St Vincent and the Grenadines have lost thousands of tourists and businesses to other Caribbean nations.

But the Caribbean Regional Airlines have filled the stop, which allow thousands of tourists and businesses to take place between Puerto Rico and St Vincent and the Grenadines.

Conversely, I believe that many people are spending their vacation in many different ways including, soaking in the sun rays on our lovely white sand beaches. This has been the trend for many decades where visitors would take a few days off from work to experience the tranquility of the tropics. This is still a tradition; however, the way people spend their vacation these days are changing.

Nowadays, hiking, attending festivals and many more are becoming the basis for people to visit our islands; therefore, we must provide the right facilities to fit these demands. The Caribbean has it all when it comes to vacationing.

Long ago, if a tropical island does not provide lovely white sand beaches its prospect of having a visitor is slim. With the changing global environment, white sand beaches no longer are the criteria for visitors to the tropics. These days, things have changed and the Caribbean have developed a diversity of environments to attract visitors.

Ideally, the Caribbean is not the only tropical destination and, more so, it is not the only place in the tropics with white sand beaches and other attractions.

In this capacity, we must not ignore the potentials of other tropical destination. Countries in Southern Asia and recently Africa are becoming tourism giants. The Caribbean needs to recognize these other destinations as fierce competitors, which would eventually take over if we don't bind our efforts. After speaking to fellow West Indians, a vast majority believes that only islands in the Caribbean have white sand beaches and spectacular attractions. In comparison, destinations such as Thailand and the Philippines have some of the best beaches in the world.

In addition, many destinations other than those of the tropics have aesthetic appeals to visitors around the world. Europe and Asia have some of the biggest names – having possessed many historical and culture ruins and sites.

I have viewed statistics about countries were international tourists mostly visit, and I have not seen a single Caribbean island on the chart. As everyone would know that Jamaica is performing the best in the Caribbean and still yet its name is nowhere close to making the top destinations. The amount of tourists visiting Jamaica annually is enormous in the eyes of Jamaicans and the rest of the region, but it is not even significant enough to be placed amongst the world's best.

After carefully accessing tourist needs I presumed that soon islands like Jamaica and the Bahamas will not experience the many tourists that swamped their shores each year. In relation to Jamaica, that nation might not be able to sustain it Travel Industry, because of the islands economic instability, coupled with the high crime rates. The same could be said about the Bahamas except that the Bahamas has a more stable economically.

Also Jamaica and the Bahamas, and the other popular destinations might not experience the high volume of tourist each year; the fact that these islands have been visited by the same people each year. People are looking for new environment and better things to do. People get weary of going to the same place too often; therefore, I predict that the unpopular islands will soon get the attention from the world.

In many online blogs many North American tourists indicated that popular destination like Jamaica and the Bahamas is not what they are seeking having gone there because of the close proximity to the Unites States. They further indicated that St Lucia and Dominica is by far prettier than the popular destinations, but the only problem, which exists, was to gather enough time to travel three hours on an airplane or overnight in another island before getting to those unpopular destinations. However, the visitors stressed that they would rather risk the over night or spend many hours of traveling than going back to any of the popular destinations in the region.

One might initiate the argument that many European countries are singled out despite the European Union. Yes! This is true, however, these European countries have enough resources to stand on their own in the Tourism Industry – I don't see the Caribbean to be in the same category.

Tourists are seeking environments, which are safe. One of the main reason for travel is to get away from the hustle and bustle in the US, Canada or Europe. Therefore, they just need some relaxation when they come to the Caribbean. No wonder why they complained if the music is pitched a little high or an ant walk across their room.

As the Director of Security at a well-established resort, one of the first questions a visitor asks "Is it safe here?" If another guest walks to close to their rooms they panic. Security is of utmost importance to them.

Year after year each Caribbean Island invests millions of dollars in campaigning for the best market share. This normally ends up in fierce competition amongst our islands. Everyone wants to advertise in well-established American Magazines, on billboard across the United States, Europe and Canada, on international television Channels such as A&E, Discovery and the Travel Channel, and through the best DVD's.

This should not be; we are supposed to come to together as a nation and deprive the rest of the world of the millions of tourist they attract each year. We could take those millions of dollars and use to advertise the region - I am sure it would be much cheaper.

The US, Europe and others are well established, because they were able to show-case their destinations especially their ecotourism sites. More so, these countries have the financial capabilities to develop these sites in whatever way they choose.

Moreover, only a few Caribbean countries have a variety of unique features. The idea here is that we all have something special to offer, if a tourist can't go to a particular Caribbean I suggest that the tourist should be referred to another Caribbean country where his or her demand can be met. This is not what is happening today, with an exception of St Lucia and St Vincent and the Grenadines that have been sharing tourists. This is a good way to start.

It is so hard to digest that Barbadians would inform tourists not to go to St Vincent and the Grenadines. I have spoken to many tourists about my country and many of them indicated that Barbadians would ask them to stay in Barbados, why go to St Vincent and the Grenadines when they have the same or even better things in Barbados. This was shocking news. We have come to the point where we start cheating the other island.

In fact, most of the tourists bound for St Vincent and the Grenadines have to in transit through Barbados before their final destination over to St Vincent and the Grenadines. The reason for this is that St Vincent and the Grenadines does not have an international airport to accommodate large jet liners.

The truth is even Vincentians passing through Barbados are facing many problems with Barbadian at their airport. The realism is that most Vincentians have to fly down to Grantley Adams International Airport before boarding a LIAT flight over to St Vincent and the Grenadines. I have experience this unwelcome behavior for myself a few times traveling back to my homeland. I was bumped off my LIAT flights and was forced to stay overnight in Barbados. In this capacity, I paid a cab to and from the airport, a hotel room for the night and food from restaurant. For the same reason I avoid Barbados as much as practicable when traveling back to my homeland.

The good thing is that I was close to home, just one hundred miles east and the bad thing about this unwelcome behavior was that I lost my seat on the flights, for no apparent reasons. For the Barbadians, this strategy is to increase revenues for the island.

The cab drivers have business and so are the hoteliers and the restaurant owners.

Being so tired on one of the many journeys there a cab driver demand a return fare to the airport from my hotel. To ensure that I get back to the airport on time the next day and considering that I had no idea how to get a cab back to the airport, I trusted the driver and paid him the fare in advance. I'd be lucky if he showed up the next day to take me back to the airport.

The Barbadian cannot be blamed for their actions, after all everyone is looking out for himself. No one told them that we were many islands under one roof. This is where our governments had to play their roles. It is time to implement the integration process within the region and stop treating each other as nothing.

I figured if St Vincent and the Grenadines were in the same position as Barbados they would have done the same or even worst. Remember that everyone is fighting for himself; there is no form of regionalism in this capacity, so why look out for the other nations.

Do not be mistaken, this is the same reason why Barbados is ranked amongst the top destinations in the region. Some tired travels destined for St Vincent and the Grenadines often end their trip in Barbados after traveling all day and having difficulties in getting on a LIAT fight to the multi-islands nation of St Vincent and the Grenadines; the tourists would not even bother to continue.

Sometimes the workers a Grantley International airport constantly inform these tourists that there is nothing enticing about St Vincent and the Grenadines, therefore, stay in Barbados where everything is beautiful and top-of-the-line. This actually works.

This makes one wonder whether these airport personnel are being trained by the authorities there.

Having assessed this behavior there is no doubt in my kind that there is no form of regionalism in the Caribbean

Evidently, I have listened to several West Indians holding many arguments. Some of the debates involve who speak best, whose island is most beautiful, which island has the most intelligent people, which island's economy is best and other similar discussion. In my opinion, we should be combining all these attributes and sell it to the world around us.

Some countries believe that they have the best strong rum, while other countries being in first place when it comes to beautiful women. It is alright to discuss these factors, but why are we trying to lift oneself and burry the other?

Let's compare ourselves to other places around the world. I believe in modeling ourselves after successful people or nations. I do admire the Americans especially; I have never heard two Americans bringing down each other states, instead they try to build the

United States of America. I realized that the US is one country, but they are identified by states, cities and towns.

To be clear, I must admit that I have heard two or more American joking about other Americans, but that where it stops.

Similarly, a person born in Nigeria will rarely tell another person that he is a Nigerian; rather he would state that he is an African. I also know that region has it conflicts, but when it comes to their well-being they often bind together to make a difference. This is hardly the case in the Caribbean. I must stress again that we are the only region separate entirely by water except in the case of Haiti and the Dominican Republic, and St Maarten and St Martin that split two different land masses.

It is my belief that vacation tourism should be heavily marketed in the region, as most islands have the facilities to accommodate vacationers. I defined vacation tourism as those tourists who come to the Caribbean to relax on the beach and staying at a hotel with exceptional service while they are being served. Most of the Islands posses this trait, except for St Vincent and the Grenadines and Dominica to some extent that is yet to be developed in that capacity – this is so when compared to other Caribbean Islands, and mainland Trinidad, which is not that rich in attracting vacationers. Haiti is in this category also.

We must unite our efforts and market these competitive advantages and differentiation strategy.

This means that countries such as the Leeward Islands, Turks and Caicos, the ABC islands, St Lucia, the Grenadines, the Bahamas, US and British Virgin Islands, Cayman Islands, Jamaica, Barbados, and other small islands can differentiate tourism as the ultimate destination for relaxing on white sand beaches at some of the top hotels in the world. Personally these islands are best suited for these kinds of vacationers. Miami Beach, in Miami, Florida; Virginia Beach in Virginia; the many white sand beaches in Thailand, Philippines and Indonesia are enticing enough in attracting more tourists than us in the Caribbean, because of two main factors – their tourist attractions are well-developed and they have more resources allotted to them in connection to advertising their destinations. To some extent these countries have more developed facilities, especially modern airports to accommodate huge commercial airlines, well-paved roads, health care, and accommodations.

This is true if you compare Indonesia, Thailand or the Philippines to islands such as St Vincent and the Grenadines and Dominica that do not have international airports, much huge inclusive hotels and upscale health facilities.

To compete against the other parts of the world the region must pursue massive and aggressive campaigns, which attracts millions of global tourist. There are some popular destinations outside of the Caribbean that we will have to take into consideration and develop the correct strategies to out-perform these other destinations.

Make no mistake that there are many European, Middle Eastern and Central American countries that are out-weighting the Caribbean. People are reverting from the tropical sensation to wanting to see historical sites - the Great Walls of China, the Pyramids of Egypt and Berlin Wall to name a few – attractions, which leave messages behind, or tell stories .

There is also the need to encourage regional traveling to sustain the region's Transportation Industry, thus maintaining the tourism industry. Europe is swamped with millions of tourists each year of which regional travelers are involved.

In recent years many tourists have been seeking other ways of spending their vacation. Instead of soaking up the rays of the sun on our many white sand beaches, a growing number of tourists are now turning to the environment for something else. More visitors are leaving their luxury suites situated on the clear turquoise waters of the Caribbean and heading to the hiking trails, animal sanctuaries, cascade waterfalls, and mountains and reefs; only a few places in the regions offer this new Caribbean getaways. This is what we called ecotourism and we should place tremendous efforts into developing this product.

The countries, which should differentiate this product, are Turks and Caicos and the Bahamas, to some extent, that have the third largest reef barrier in the world, Dominica that is known as the nature islands of the Caribbean, Trinidad and Tobago that host the famous Caroni swamp, Antigua and Barbuda with its bird sanctuary, St Vincent and the Grenadines that host a number of nature trails, a caves, an active volcano, forests and many waterfalls, and Guyana that has the world renown Amazon forest. There are many other magnificent places to see in the Caribbean to differentiate from our competitors.

Do not get me wrong there many other Caribbean Islands with a little of everything. The differentiation strategy means that islands that are not so strong in ecotourism must still make awareness, but the effort and money should be placed on areas where there are most strong and vice versa.

Ecotourism also attracts people who are socially and ecologically conscious minded. These people have enormous interest in researching the environment; mostly where fauna, flora and cultural history are rich.

Comparatively, I do not think that each Caribbean Islands could hold their own, in this aspect. We have many competitors around the world as it relates to ecotourism. It is true that many of our islands posses these breath taking nature's desires. Many people are not aware of the many ecotourism attractions outside of the Caribbean Region. These sites are well developed and millions of dollars are being spent to upgrade and maintain these places.

Each year millions of international tourists leave their homes and travel to various parts of the world. Some of the most popular attractions are found in Europe; Paris, France have accommodated more than seventy million tourists each year. The Grand Canal in Venice, Italy also secured a name for itself, having catered for millions of tourists from around the world. Other places such as, Niagara Falls in Canada and the United States and Madame Tussauds in London, England are internationally recognized and they have enticed millions of people every year.

With the resources, which are available to these countries outside of the region, the leaders of the Caribbean must be inventive and innovative and develop new ideas, which would create a name beyond those found elsewhere.

There is another form of tourism, which I called leisure tourism that I would like to see as a single movement in the Caribbean – again let us do some specialization; build on what we have the competitive edge in. Trinidad and Tobago carnival is one of the well known carnivals in the world. I hope I am not exaggerating here, but everywhere I go people always refer to *"Trini carnival,"* Whether it is in Canada, England, United States, or even people from different parts of the world who I have come into contact with.

In fact, many Caribbean islands boast about their Carnival and they indicated that their carnival is comparative to Trinidad and Tobago's carnival. In my honest opinion, this is a statement beyond being false.

The only two other carnivals in the regions recognized by tourist are Barbados' Crop Over and "Vincy Carnival" in St Vincent and the Grenadines.

Trinidad and Tobago Carnival is more organized, better attended and more colorful than the other carnivals including Barbados' Crop Over and St Vincent and the Grenadines "*Vincy* Carnival"

Let us build and advertise *Junkanoo* Festival in the Bahamas – for the people who are not familiar with *Junkanoo*, it is a street parade and a rich cultural festival mostly known to Bahamians and adopted by the people of the Turks and Caicos Islands that have close association with the culture of the Bahamas. It is also similar to carnival in the streets of Trinidad and Tobago.

There is also the need to enhance and market the Jazz festival in St Lucia, which is one of the biggest events occurring in the West Indies. The Jazz Festival has acclaimed worldwide scrutiny.

Let's move a bit further south to St Vincent and the Grenadines famous the "Nine Mornings" festivities - a festival, which is unique to the local people there. The Nine Mornings Festival is where local people wake at early mornings – starting from the ninth morning leading up to Christmas - to celebrate, through street parties and dance to music until the dawn of the morning. It runs from December 16 to December 25 each year. This cultural expression has escalated into one of the best festival in St Vincent and the Grenadines, having out-performed the local "*Vincy Carnival*" in terms of attendances and revenues.

Another unique festival in St Vincent and the Grenadines is the "Nine-and-we-and-them," a Christmas ceremonial from various organizations on the island. This show had out-performed all other gatherings in the history of St Vincent and the Grenadines. I assumed it is part of the Nine Mornings Festivals. The nine morning festivals have attracted a far bigger crowd in that country – compared to other gathering including One Day International cricket at Arnos Vale, Ms Carnival contestant show at Victoria Park, Independence Day parade at Victoria Park and "Vincy Carnival" Tuesday parade also at Victoria Park.

I must stress the Reggae song splash in Jamaica has drawn attention from many parts of the world. The Reggae song splash brings the entire Reggae family together on one stage. This has attracted thousands of people.

Lastly, we must promote the Creole Festivals in Guadeloupe, Martinique, Dominica and St Lucia, where cultural traditions, based on French presence in those islands, are transformed and showcased.

There are other festivals through- out the Caribbean which we could assess and developed. The Caribbean in itself is rich in many aspects and we must come together to upgrade and market this unique fraction of the world.

Furthermore, there is a need to promote education tourism. If we are going to linked in this capacity, we must learned about each other islands in a way to enhance our knowledge of the similarities and differences in our cultures, languages and other aspects of our lives. The Eastern Caribbean has initiated this idea, where they have students exchange programs. At least Vincentian students traveled to Martinique and Venezuela each year in an effort to enhance students' abilities to speak French and Spanish respectively. Also I have seen within the Turks and Caicos Islands where students travel to the Dominican Republic on field trips to enhance their knowledge about that country and the Spanish Language.

We must learn about the Spanish ruins in Cuba and the Dominican Republic; the French ruins in Haiti,

Martinique and Guadeloupe, the Dutch ruins in the Netherlands Antilles, and the many British ruins in the Eastern Caribbean and the rest of the English speaking Caribbean. We must learn and visit all the nature and hiking trails, volcanoes in Montserrat and St Vincent and the Grenadines, the Sulfur Springs in Dominica and St Lucia and many other sites.

In fact, the people in the Bahamas do not possess much knowledge about the Eastern Caribbean and vice versa. There are people in the Eastern Caribbean who have never heard about the Turks and Caicos and vice versa. Personally, it is only recently I have learnt about St Barth. Our people have to be educated – let's educate them.

West Indians are obliged to know why islands like St Lucia and Dominica speak English and the Creole Languages.

We need to know the reason why Grenada is called the Spice Island.

There is the need to educate citizens the reason why St Vincent and the Grenadines is called the Land of the Blessed and why it hosted the oldest Botanical Gardens in the west. These islands were also known as

Hairouna - why was the name changed to St Vincent and the Grenadines.

St Kitts and Nevis was St Christopher and Nevis and why the name was changed

St Lucia was called the Helen of the West – there is a lot to learn about each other.

This idea will also allow us to improve our scientific competence outside of the classroom.

Some individual islands do not even have the enough resources to sustain, develop, or even market their attractions. In this capacity, we must pool all our resources together and market the Caribbean and no effort should be made to market a single island.

Ideally, we should provide some medium of diverse transportation and infrastructure to the other parts of the Caribbean, whether it is by air or sea. To illustrate this new idea, if tourists who are vacationing in St Vincent and the Grenadines want to see the lush Piton in Vieux Forth, St Lucia they should be able to have a quick flight with a helicopter or some form of quick water taxi. If visitors in St Kitts and Nevis want to visit the Volcano in Montserrat, they could be provided with similar service.

Let us look at the global competition in this area. There are many festivities around the world, which we have to compete against. When we develop an area we must do it in a way that tourist will discard the competitor and follow what have been developed in the region. We have to be mindful of festivities like Brazil carnival, the most renowned carnival in the world, which attracts many people from all over the globe. Another well-known carnival is the Louisiana Mardi Gras in Louisiana, United States. Also is the well-attended Labor Day Parade in Manhattan in New York. The ironic thing about this it that this festivity is a planned tradition of a combination of several Caribbean Islands; Trinidad and Tobago, Jamaica, St Vincent and the Grenadines and Barbados to name a few. It is in my interest to make mention of Caribana festival, which attracts millions of people to Toronto city year by year.

Caribana is also a Caribbean culture and tradition in Toronto, Canada and attracts more than one million tourists each summer and it is responsible for bringing in more than two hundred million dollars into Ontario economy.

If a few West Indians living in Toronto created such world renowned festival within little or no resources, just imagine what we can do in the region with more available resources and leadership.

There are other attractions that we could implement; a modern day museum, which depicts our rich history. This will educate us about our past present and future, and visitors alike.

Our governments should create a digital illustration of different parts of the history; showing for example, the Middle Passage phenomenon; Christopher Columbus' arrival with the Nina, Pinta and Santa Maria ships; the era of slavery; the cultures of the local Carib Indian and so on.

Everyone is interested in history and culture regardless of the person's backgrounds and temperaments.

Tourism has contributed well to the economies of the Caribbean. However, I believe that we could do even better if we integrate our tourism sectors. One may ask how I knew all these facts, but as a citizen of the West Indies I am always keeping abreast of what is happening.

Recent trends indicated that the tourism industry in the Caribbean had been on the decline, thus, a declined in global market share starting from 911 terrorist attacks on United States of America.

We must place extra effort on islands that are not so popular. In fact, the only popular islands in the Caribbean other than the more developed countries are Grenada, Antigua and Barbuda, the Virgin Islands, Cayman Islands and St Lucia to some extent. Many tourists have not heard about most of the lesser developed countries and most of them cannot even locate these islands on the world map.

The Netherlands Antilles, which are Curacao, Bonaire and Aruba; the French West Indies being Martinique and Guadeloupe; and Montserrat that gained some world attention when the island's volcano erupted a few years ago.

Combining the regions tourism will enhance the amount of travelers in the Cruise Industry and the number of international and regional flights to the islands. This is consequent to increased awareness, sharing of visitors and development of facilities within the region. Increased visitors' arrival means more revenues for the region.

Ideally, employment is a sure thing. Increase in the number of arrivals suggests that more facilities will be needed to accommodate this increase, therefore, jobs will be provided. The construction industry will escalate; the service industry will have to employ more people as tours guides and other hotel and tourism operations.

I would like to see much more effort into research and Development. We need to know where our tourists will come from and what each tourist is interested in. We do not want to market a destination, which only have white sand beaches to tourists who are interested in nature trails and hiking, or market to entire product to random target markets.

It must be highlighted that Research and Development is an expensive process, but it identifies the specific areas where, how, when, why and what we should advertised a particular product – we should make awareness of a particular product, or service in which a particular set of people have interest.

In an effort to satisfy our guests, we must also develop the technology around us. We have to attract low cost airlines and we must create travel packages to our visitors. We must have affordable and efficient Internet services and improved hotel accommodations.

Furthermore a safe environment must be provided for our customers. A well-established security system is needed against crimes like rape, kidnap, burglary, robbery and theft should be implemented.

Through satisfaction we must promote sustainable tourism. As a nation we must be committed to create low impact on the environment - physical environment, which includes the natural environment and the construction environment, which recently escalated in many islands in the region and the biological life; and the local culture. One of my recent professors defined culture, "Culture is everything," he rightly claimed. It is people's beliefs, behavior, preferred taste in humanities, fine arts, values, attitudes and goals. Sustainable tourism in this sense is also important in creating employment for local communities, therefore, providing an income. The main goal for sustainable tourism is to make sure that development is created in a positive path for local communities, the tourists themselves and the companies that service the Tourism Industry.

The impact of tourism is evident everywhere throughout the region, but not so much for St Vincent and the Grenadines and Dominica where a hand-full of tourists visit those islands each year. If we practice sustainable tourism we are able to eliminate the impact of tourism in many ways, which includes enhancing regional economies through the purchases of goods and services from small businesses. In doing so, they must also educate themselves about regional politics, economies and cultures.

Two aspects of sustainable tourism the Caribbean must focus on are bird watching and whale watching. We must place more effort in learning pelagic bird migration flyways. In winters birds migrate from the Arctic to the warmer areas of the tropics - hundreds of species at once. These birds have specific pathways from their journeys in the north. Some flights occur in different areas - like the birds that leaves Nova Scotia and Labrador in Canada fly down over the Atlantic Ocean and into the Caribbean, before they continue their journey into South America. There is also a time when they would return to the Arctic during the summer season. We should be educated toward this in an effort to educate our visitors.

Bird watching plays a big role in attracting tourist arrivals to the region. Some of our islands, specifically Dominica, Dominican Republic, Haiti, Jamaica, Cuba and St Vincent and the Grenadines that possess sustained habitat for bird, have a large number of bird species.

Bird watching is also unique in the sense that each island has a national bird. Some Eastern Caribbean Islands have different species of the parrot that is special to each island. However, recent statistics indicate that these bird species are becoming fewer in number.

The decline has been affected by many factors. The region is bombarded by many natural disasters the most significant being hurricanes, erosion from heavy rain falls and most recently, volcanic actions.

Natural disasters destroy natural habitats for birds; therefore, they migrate in an effort to find another home.

Tourists also play a part in the decline of our bird species. Many locals are catching and selling these birds to tourists who take them back to their various homes.

When these disasters occur in one area of the Caribbean, visitors can be diverted to other parts of the Caribbean, while the habits for these birds are being rejuvenated. The way our tourism is operated is that if one island cannot accommodate its visitors the visitors won't be directed to another Caribbean Islands, which has similar recreation.

Whale watching is another phenomenon. The Turks and Caicos Islands are famous for its whales watching in Grand Turk and Salt Cay. Whales do visit these shores from February to April each year. These whales move between Grand Turk and the Silver Banks of the Dominican Republic. Whale watching facilities have also developed throughout the islands - Grenada, St Lucia, Dominica, St Vincent and the Grenadines and St Kitts and Nevis.

There are many other islands, which have potentials in making a name for the Caribbean; Saba, St Bath and neighboring islands in the Northern Caribbean.

Tourism is important to the region; therefore, we must put more combined effort in sustaining it.

One would remember the wake of 911 in New York. The world all over was affected in all aspects whether it was through sports, tourism, economies and education. For a many days the airports throughout the United States were closed, creating enormous losses in the United States and around the world.

Recently, the global recession has caused significant declines in the Tourist Industry including visitors to the Caribbean. In the northern Caribbean mainly Turks and Caicos, The Bahamas, Cayman Islands and Cuba were severely affected, since these islands mainly have tourists from North America. In the southern Caribbean, however, in island such as Barbados, St Lucia and Antigua and Barbuda, many of the visitors come from Europe.

Other issues, which affects the tourism industry whether in the Caribbean or worldwide are wars, influenza and other economic crisis. The region could be ready for all this, only if they remove the competitive barriers within the region itself.

In light of this, these factors would not affect us so badly if we were operating under one umbrella. When one area is affected the other area will be there as a substitute. In times of damages the building back process is quicker and easier.

Many islands in the Caribbean might be aware of this; however, because they are doing extremely well in the tourism sector, and in other areas of their operations, they might not be willing to integrate their tourism.

I have many debates with people from different parts of the Caribbean and the Bahamians, Turks Islanders, some Jamaicans and US and British Virgin Islanders and their opinions toward an integration of the Caribbean. The majority of them think it not a good idea. I am also assuming that the Cayman Islands would not want to be part of the integration process, since their tourism sector and their economy are doing well compared to other Caribbean Islands.

The reason for their decline – not to say the same about the Cayman Islands, is that they don't need to link their tourism sector when they are doing far better than some islands; hence, they are better-off operating alone.

My argument is that Islands like the Bahamas, Cayman Islands, British and US Virgin Islands, Turks and Caicos and Antigua and Barbuda's to some extent, where these economies are not that diverse to sustain those countries; there might be economic ramifications in the event the travel industry is suspended for some apparent reason.

At travel summits, it pains to see that all the islands are competing against each other; making awareness of how beautiful and first class an individual islands is. I believe that strategy is the wrong direction we are heading – as we should be making awareness through a unified Caribbean against the rest of the Globe.

There is no question in my mind that the notion of individualism amongst Caribbean Islands has influenced the idea of limiting the free movements of people from other Caribbean Islands through Visa application. Citizens from Haiti and the Dominican Republic have to be in possession of a visitors' visa to visit everywhere in the Caribbean, including the Bahamas and Turks and Caicos Islands. Jamaicans have to apply for visitors' Visa to the Bahamas and the Turks and Caicos. I have little knowledge about the Cayman Islands, but they are free to travel to the Eastern Caribbean without a Visa.

We cannot be integrated if we are being restricted by Visa, there must be free movements of the people. Let's take a lesson from the Americans and the Europeans, where there citizens travel freely.

This lack of vision also defeats our tourism and travel industry; restricting the free movements of the people. In Europe, the Europeans are free to travel across borders without visa restrictions.

I also guarantee that if we unite or tourism sector we will grow two-fold from increases advertisements, differentiation strategy, Research and Development, and shared ideas.

We must take into consideration the product mix when we are marketing our islands. This is certainly a multi-faceted process and it is a continuous one. The Caribbean must establish a tourism committee that will research the potential consumers, products and markets, and making awareness through advertising through the media.

First, we must set prices, which meet our needs and the needs of the visitors; sometime we may create packages, which will suit the consumers needs. The price, however, will vary according to consumer needs and wants.

Second is the promotion of the product or service. In this, capacity, we have to make awareness through a variety of media such as, billboard, magazines, newspaper, radio, television, DVD, flyers and the newest advertising medium, the Internet. In essence, promotion is defining the destination. Let me stress that word-of-mouth is one of the most powerful tools in making awareness. People often tell others whether their vacation experience was good or bad, therefore, potential visitors will decide whether they will buy the product or services.

Third, is the place or what some social scientist term as distribution. This involves the channels and agencies, which allow access to purchase our products and services, hence, the reason for the many travel agents around the world; yacht and cruise ships companies, airlines companies, hoteliers and tours guides.

Last, is product, which the consumer buys. This is the actual attributes of the product itself, its packaging and branding. A brand is created upon the quality of the product and the service it provides.

Personally, I don't believe in a St Vincent and the Grenadines, Bahamas or Grenada brand or package, instead I am interested in a Caribbean brand, with packages to St Vincent and the Grenadines, Bahamas or Grenada, which will make a global impact. The fact remains that no single island in the Caribbean has enough product or service to create a brand for itself.

This integration strategy is also relevant, since it will enable the region to work smarter. This ideology creates consistent and coherent approach, which is focused on the implementation and decision making and reduce cost while focusing on the agility of prospective business.

According to business, the environment overtime will reduce total cost of ownership and provide return on investment. However, the drawbacks of the integration theory could be that different project might require different technology and facilities.

In our eyes the brand is individual countries; it is true — every island in the region rightly called themselves Gem of the Antilles, but with the wrong motive of developing themselves. Maybe we should call ourselves the Gem of the West.

The truth is we have not created a brand for ourselves, the tourists have. We called it St Vincent and the Grenadines and Jamaica and the like, but the tourists called it the Caribbean — we should take this lesson from them.

Some tourists identify our islands as the travel destination for the rich and famous. I could vow for Mustique islands in St Vincent and the Grenadines, West Caicos in the Turks and Caicos Islands, New Providence Islands in the Bahamas — these are some of the playgrounds and get-away for the rich and the famous. Surprisingly, the competition is fierce, where the rich and the famous are now vacationing in the African Safari, Paris, France, Dubai, and other Middle Eastern countries.

They also view the islands as having a plethora of festivals, tropical forests, hypnotic rhythms and delicious cuisines of all kinds mainly French and local cuisines. The Caribbean according to them is a place of relax and romantic getaway – in short the region is the ultimate vacation paradise.

From a tourism point of view we have continuous work ahead of us. A committee must be set up to deal with this integration process and to see that it is maintained. This should be in the best interest of the region and not individual countries.

Tourism plays a vital role in our economies and we must protect it. We cannot, however, match up with the rest of the world if we try to confront them individually, therefore, we must come together to combat the issues and develop our region.

The Caribbean is nothing without tourism and the region is nothing without each other – let's start the journey together.

Meeting the world as individual teams cannot be maintained. If so, we are doing it to compete among ourselves, to market ourselves as a single islands. Do we want to tell the world that you can come to St Vincent and the Grenadines and see our beautiful, famous Botanical gardens, or our breath-taking Duns river waterfalls in Jamaica, or we want to tell the world once you visit the cascading water Falls of Beleine in St Vincent and the Grenadines you must visit the lust Pitons in St Lucia, the magnificent and crystallized Harrison Cave of Barbados, the three hundred and sixty five sparkling fresh water rivers flowing from the lust rainforests in Dominica, to the three hundred and sixty five white sand beaches in Antigua, which are surrounded by clear pristine waters.

The world is running away from us while we are competing amongst ourselves. The great barrier is still attracting millions of tourist each year and Niagara Falls is doing even better.

Our leaders must not waste any more time trying to find ways to steal each other tourists, but time and energy, and other resources should be in place to develop an extensive combined strategy against the rest of the world.

If we don't start now, we'll lose the chance of ever becoming competitive.

~ **PART 4** ~

Safety and Security

The past leaders of the Organization for Eastern Caribbean States-OECS-members' states should be applauded for their vision, which our present leaders are failing to conceptualize. The world over will soon becomes a single unit, where every region is forming alliances in all aspects, including that of security and safety. In this sense, it is necessary that the Caribbean introduces and implements a regional police force.

The Eastern Caribbean has always faceted integration, but their efforts were crippled and discouraged by the so-called More Developed Countries, especially Jamaica and Barbados that have economic differences and disputes. The Regional Security System - the RSS that was created by the OECS is closest the region has come to creating oneness for our security and safety.

As part of our effort to secure our nation we must established a regional police force. There is no doubt in my mind that we need such a force within the region considering the many crimes against humanity.

Furthermore, the Caribbean has become a safe haven for criminals from other parts of the globe - criminals who have committed crimes at home have used the Caribbean as a hide out from the law.

I must commend the Eastern Caribbean along with Barbados for their vision of creating the Regional Security Systems - the RSS - with head quarters at the paragon Center in Barbados. It is true that most of the eastern Caribbean Islands encourage a one nation notion. Again I believe that the Caribbean should be integrated through a one region police force.

Security itself is becoming increasingly challenging, where the focus is placed on physical security. Conceivable threats can develop from many sources and hierarchies in societies, domestic or from an international environment. The purpose for constructing a regional security system is to prevent the out-burst of conflict throughout the region.

In recent years globalization has created a joint world, thereby, positioning the world as a global back yard for everyone. I often picture the Caribbean as a border less region where boundaries are of no importance. The new phenomenon is globalization where the world is binding in many aspects - trade, economy, sports, and the like. I believe that if the Caribbean is to become part of the global family they must first regionalize.

Our islands are, according to global standards are poor developing countries, which cannot support themselves in many ways. Some countries and institution refer to the Caribbean as third world countries. Moreover, none of our islands is economically viable enough to be classed a first world country. The United States, for example, which is the most powerful country in the world, by far, has joined force with other countries, such as Canada and Mexico and many European, African, Asian and Latin American countries to form the United Nations – a force that protects the world.

Furthermore there are many powerful nations in Europe that has created massive arm forces to protect the interest of the European Union and the World when the need arises. It is obvious that there is a positive impact from regionalism and we should sit down as head of states and citizens, and discuss these positive impacts to initiate some form of stability within the region. It worked for Europe, United States and Asia; therefore, the Caribbean is no exception.

These days the Caribbean has become a hot spot. West Indians are committing more crimes subsequent to increase economic instability which leads to drug trafficking, arm robberies, murder, kidnapping, thefts and burglaries.

This is mostly evident in Jamaica, Haiti, the Dominican Republic, Guyana, and Trinidad and Tobago.

Quickly, the smaller Islands of the Caribbean, which include the Eastern Caribbean Islands, are becoming victims of relentless crimes. Because of the economic problems in the United States and Europe, and the global recession, many Caribbean Islands that depend heavily on tourism have lost many hotel and tourism related jobs; hence, the increase in crimes.

Recently, in the Turks and Caicos Islands arm robberies has escalated, resulted in many deaths. The

Bahamas is being terrorized by many crimes at the beginning of the 2010.

The RSS has been created to respond to any threats within the Eastern Caribbean. This vision was influenced by ongoing security threats within the region starting from the 1970's. Moreover, the RSS were initially created by the United States to fight the influence of Communism in the Caribbean - just in time to assist in the 1983 Grenada invasion by the United States.

However, since the establishment of the RSS there were many crises, which the international agreement has responded to. Some of these crises include the Grenada Invasion, Hurricane Hugo in Antigua and Barbuda and the coup d'etat in Port of Spain, Trinidad and Tobago. This means that, although Trinidad and Tobago is not a part of the RSS, the organization had seen it fit support its neighbor in difficult times.

It is evident that the region has been plagued by a number of crisis and, therefore, we need our own forces to respond to any security threats to the islands. I recommend that the Regional Security System keeps its name and strengthened with manpower, weapons and equipments from across the region.

Jamaica, Antigua and Barbuda, the Bahamas, Trinidad and Tobago are in good position to promote this new idea, since they have already created their own defense forces.

My suggestion is that the Regional Security System be equipped with more than three hundred and fifty thousand men and women from the Caribbean Islands. The region host almost seventy millions people and enough arm forces have to be in place to deal with at least eleven million people at once and being able to confront more than one crisis at the same time.

Moreover, we must prepare to assist the rest of the world to fight crimes and other crises alongside NATO, UN and British and United Kingdom arm forces.

We must, however, equip these forces with the right tools to be effective in getting the job done. Enough weapons and ammunition must be in supply and the right armored vehicles as a form of protection against the enemies. Military boats and helicopters must be purchased to be able to operate from air and sea, considering the topography of most Caribbean Islands.

Therefore, there is a need to seek help from the international community; countries such as the United States of America, Japan, Australia and many European Counties in providing military assistance; money, weapons, ammunitions and training.

There are many lessons to be learnt from other regional forces throughout the world – from the United Nations and NATO.

But the regional force, which best describe our region is the Royal Canadian Mounted Police - RCMP. The RCMP is the Canadian national police force. Its basic responsibility is to ensure that federal laws are maintained throughout all provinces in Canada. The RCMP also operates internationally to divert criminal activities against Canada. The organization has set up liaison officers in many countries around the world for investigation purposes and to seek out intelligence to be effective and efficient when fighting crimes against the state.

The idea here is to benchmark this arm force and adapt their daily operation.

I would like to see the regional force set up as a paramilitary force for the Caribbean. The meaning of paramilitary varies according to who is presenting the idea; however, my idea about the subject is to position us so that our forces could respond to national threats, which include hostility, rebels and crimes within the state.

The Dominican Republic, Haiti, Guyana, Puerto Rico and Jamaica already have some defense equipments, which they can either trade or sell to the new police force. These islands already developed noticeable small arm forces - a defense force as they called it.

Bases should be in Hispaniola at the border of the Dominican Republic, which will serve the northern Caribbean nations from the Bahamas to Puerto Rico and Cuba. The location between at the border of the Dominican Republic and Haiti is also ideal when you look at the many conflicts in that part of the region, which include Jamaica. Ideally, another base should be located in Trinidad and Tobago to combat the many conflicts there and to serve the entire Eastern Caribbean including the British and US Virgin Islands.

There are also small forces within the Eastern Caribbean. National defense is normally up held by the local police force, which has a small force called the Special Services Unit – the SSU. Moreover, in times where the problem is too extensive for the local force the RSS will commit to assisting with security.

The islands have their own problems, some of are easily solved problems and other islands have difficult and ongoing problems. Let me discuss some of the problems face throughout the Caribbean.

Let us start with Trinidad and Tobago, the twin island republic and it is the southern most Caribbean Island, which lies northeast of Venezuela and south of Grenada. According to my knowledge the islands are more than nineteen hundred square miles in area. They are English speaking and their economy is primarily industrial. These two islands have a population around two million. Mainland Trinidad boasts the natural petroleum gas, which is being mined and exported. Last, the islands are known for its Carnival, soca and steel pan music.

Trinidad and Tobago have an ongoing crime problem. To date Trinidad and Tobago ranked high in kidnapping crimes, where people of status in society are targeted and a ransom is demanded by the kidnapper. During the time I lived in Toronto, Canada in 2006, the Royal Canadian Mounted Police had gone to Trinidad and Tobago to assist with major crimes there. The islands is also demised by many relentless crimes, especially gang related murders, which was on the rise since 1998. In my view, crimes in Trinidad is consequent to the unstable economic and political problem in that twin island republic.

There are also many gun related crimes especially on mainland Trinidad; many visitors and residence feared these on-going crimes.

Not withholding the horrendous attempted coup d'etat in 1990 staged by Yasin Abu Bakr of Trinidad and Tobago. After following the news around that time Abu Bakr known by most West Indians was born as Lennox Philips and it was shocking to find out that he is a former police man on that island. News also revealed that Abu Bakr was converted to Islam during his tenure at a Canadian University where he studied.

Yasin Abu Bakr attempt lasted a few days before the arm forces in Trinidad and Tobago regained control over the state. The fear was that if Abu Bakr, as addressed by most people in the Caribbean, had more followers at his exposure his attempt to over throw the government would be a successful one. Much credit must be given to the Regional Security System that assisted so generously.

Interestingly, in 2005 there were a series of four bombings in downtown Port of Spain. One would know that Port of Spain is an extremely busy city with close to fifty thousand people living there. In any day about a quarter of a million people commuted through the large bustling city; a place with hundreds of shopping centers. According to news reports out of Trinidad and Tobago, these accused persons were never found nor were their motives identified – is this, an act of terrorism? I hope not, as one could only stipulate.

In St Vincent and the Grenadines there was much fear, as many Vincentians have families in Trinidad and Tobago. Many Vincentians had gone to Trinidad and Tobago during the Eric Williams' era. To be exact many of my families had migrated there during that time. Everyone in St Vincent listened attentively to what was happening on mainland Trinidad – our beloved neighbor.

According to the news - NBC radio, the lone radio station in St Vincent and the Grenadines that time, Abu Bakr and company had gone into the Red House and held Prime Minister A.N.R Robinson and other ministers of Parliament hostage. The news also exclaimed that Abu Bakr and his men had fired many shots at the Red House.

These gun shots were still visible at the time I visited Trinidad and Tobago in 1996 for the first time.

I wondered what would be Abu Bakr's next move and what the regional leaders were planning to do about it.

It is obvious that nothing much was done, since the region fourteen years later still does not have an equipped regional police force.

The negotiation lasted for several days, after which Abu Bakr and others were taken into custody. This was the first time I knew Trinidad and Tobago has a defense force of its own to secure the people of the two islands state. The news also highlighted that many citizens looted the city of Port of Spain during that time and I believe a few people were killed during the attempt to overthrow the government.

To my bad memory, I can't recall if the United States had sent in their troops in an effort to help regain control of the island. It could be that the local defense force and the police service were well equipped and capable of regaining control over their state. However, the economy was not that unstable, hence, the government was able to provide and train an effective defense and police forces. I am not sure if I could say the same today about the twin island state.

To date I do not understand the attempt to overthrow the Trinidad and Tobago government.

But I know that these are time when we need the service of a regional force.

Let's turn our focus on Grenada, the one hundred and thirty square miles islands and a small population around one hundred thousand, located north of Trinidad and Tobago ad south of St Vincent and the Grenadines. Grenada is also known as the Spice Isle because of its mass production of spices. However, I believe that the Spice Isle has gained world wide attention when the United States Arm Forces invaded the islands under the Ronald Reagan presidency.

In 1983, while I was playing with friends in my Grandmother front yard I heard and saw the noise of two black jets, scotching the sky over us. These planes were flying at very low altitude and just above the windward coastline of St Vincent and the Grenadines. We were just around nine years old and too young to know what was happening around us. Back then we never listened to the news on the radio, nor did we have television to even look at CNN news.

However, from time to time I heard the news over the radio and listened to the older folks while they spoke about the uprising.

From my understanding, the United States invasion in Grenada was subsequent to a number of Cuban officials, who were setting up a Communist state government. The Prime Minister of Grenada at the time was Maurice Bishop who overthrew the Eric Gairy's government through an armed revolution, thus, suspended the constitution of Grenada. Maurice Bishop was later executed during the rivalry.

There is no need to discuss the entire invasion of the islands, but what is important is how the island was secured after the overthrowing of the government. Many years after I would watch the whole story on the History channel.

I would find out that many forces assisted the Americans including our own Regional Security Services, and which included the Eastern Caribbean, Barbados' defense force and Jamaica's force, amongst some other battalions.

It was good in part of the Americans to intervene, but again it was in the best interest of the

Americans to stop the spread Communism within the region and moreover, the entire globe.

Our regional forces, which involve Jamaica and the RSS, had also done us proud. This shows that we are cable of getting the job done. Therefore, let's build on that experience and form our own alliances to combat breach of national security like the overthrowing of the Grenada government in 1983.

I had the privilege to work alongside some of the brave policemen who had been sent to Grenada and survived the horrendous acts carried out by the many officials in Grenada at the time.

The big question is suppose that stopping the spread of Communist was not in the best interest of the Americans, what would happen to Grenada? The answer is simple. It is either that the Americans won't invade the island or would delay its operations for months if not years.

We have to stop waiting and begging for things to be one in our backyard. We have to take the initiative and do it ourselves. Doing it ourselves means that we have to build our own regional force.

There is no doubt that if we had a regional force that Cuba will be in the state it is today. What pains me so much about the Cuban scenario is that after forty years of a painstaking Fidel Castro regime, he handed over power to his brother – where is the right of the people to choose a leader through democracy?

Cuba is the largest island in area and the most populous in the Caribbean. The island has total area of more than forty two thousand square miles and home to about eleven million people. It is Spanish in origin and only ninety miles south of Miami, Florida – about the same distance between St Vincent and the Grenadines and Barbados. It is the only Communist state in the region.

Cuba has a similar history to Grenada attempt to make the Spice Island a Communist state. There are many similarities coupled with many differences. However, one of the differences between the two is that Fidel Castro and his followers has succeeded and subsequently, still administering power in Cuba today.

Nowadays many of us sympathize with the people of Cuba and wish we could just change what is happening to them. Forty years under the United States door step and nothing had been done.

We must employ security and safety, and encourage democracy amongst our neighbors, in particular, while simultaneously redo ourselves as a model of Caribbean regionalism.

How much longer can we wait before our neighbors are free?

While on the topic of Communism, it was rumored that the Prime Minister of St Vincent and the Grenadines had recently tried to change the constitution of the multi-island nation in an effort to instill Communism. During that time I followed the local media in St Vincent and the Grenadines, which purported that there were much tension between the Unity Labor Party and the New Democratic Party. The government had called an election for citizen to vote on the referendum of the new constitution on November 26, 2009. I had the privilege to listen to the results live on one of the many radio stations on the island.

Had the people of St Vincent and the Grenadines decided to create problems I often wonder where the security would come from, when the size of the local police force is taken into consideration.

According to sources in on the mainland, members from the Venezuela's military were often seen in St Vincent and the Grenadines. Had this military decided to take over, we have no force in the Caribbean, or even if they are combined, to match the well-equipped Venezuelan military.

The New Democratic Party in St Vincent and the Grenadines reminded the people of the Invasion of Grenada back in 1983. Vincentians were also reminded of the loss of freedom if Communism is introduced to the state.

Conversely, I could not end this topic without making mention of Haiti, another country, which has a difficult past.

Haiti is one of the countries on Hispaniola with a native Creole Language. The Country is more than ten thousand square mile in area, making it the third largest in the Caribbean, and a population just over ten million. Some good things to learn about Haiti are that this country was the first country in the West to gain independence through revolution. It was also the first country in the Caribbean to be qualified for the world cup games in 1974.

After a hot day on the parade square at the Old Montrose Police Training School, in St Vincent and the Grenadines, I began to slick my shoes and starch my uniform for parade the following day. It was about two months into my police training and the members of the Special Services Unit, which is located on the same compound, were preparing to be deployed to Haiti.

At this time the only thing I had known about Haiti was that the country was very poor and it was known for practicing witchcraft rituals. Corporal Hazelwood and I spoke briefly about his mission to Haiti. After hearing about the mission I wanted to sign up for combat mission but I was only two months into my six months course - I was not ready for that kind of mission. More so, I had not even learned to use any form of firearm. Weeks later, I sadly, watched the Special Services Unit team departed the compound on their way to Haiti.

Again, I do not wish to explain what happened, but the fact remained that another Caribbean Island had domestic problems and we have to wait for the United States and other international forces to initiate the intervention. Had a regional force established we could have move in first and if other international forces want to follow then we we'll gladly welcome them.

Haiti needs our help with its ongoing civil unrests. To date the United Nation is still occupying the country; trying to bring peace to the country's ten million residents.

This was another significant appearance for the forces in the region, in particular the RSS and members from the Trinidad and Tobago and Jamaica defense forces.

There are many other crisis, which the region had experience and our regional forces have been contributing in a significant way to the Eastern Caribbean and rest of the region.

Other parts of the Caribbean have not experience such horrible coup d'état like those in Grenada, Trinidad and Tobago, Haiti and Cuba. Each year the islands are plagued by hurricanes – the hurricane season is between June and November. Islands like Antigua and Barbuda had been severely devastated by hurricane Hugo and Luis in 1989 and 1995 respectively; and Hurricane Marilyn that devastated St Kitts and Nevis in 1995, acclaimed millions of dollars in damages.

In other islands like Barbados, St Kitts and Nevis and St Lucia that have had uprising of inmates at their local prisons. In the case of St Lucia, this island had once had to transfer prison inmates from one facility to another.

A regional force should be in place to deal with these dangerous situations and to assist in the aftermath of the dreadful Hurricanes.

But this is not all; Jamaica is hampered by thousands of crimes each year, mostly associated with drugs and the instability of the local economy. In Jamaica almost every house has to be barricaded with burglar bars, to keep out burglars.

In my three weeks in Spanish Town, Jamaica in 2000, at least four people; three civilians and one police officer or soldier is killed each day – every scary if you were in Jamaica at the time these horrible crimes are committed.

The harvesting and trading of marijuana has been a continuous problem in that state. Trading marijuana is a trade and the people consume marijuana as though it is part of their lives – more so, they smoke on streets one would think it's an ordinary product in the market.

The local police force and the defense force have tried to calm the situation with no success. According to reports there have been a huge number of the corrupted law enforcement officers, therefore, there is a problem for the officers who want to see justice done. In light of this, it appears as though the local forces there are incapable of detecting crimes on the island, hence, incapable of solving them.

Where is our regional force when we need it?

In addition, because of the relentless crimes on the island it present threats to tourists. If we are going to regionalize our Travel Industry, places like Jamaica must be dealt with.

This is also an ongoing problem in the state. Jamaica is known to having one of the highest murder rates in the world – shocking reports. The Caribbean is supposed to be a quiet place where people come to relax. In 2005 the island had the highest murder rate throughout the globe. We often ask ourselves how cans a tiny island, when compared to countries like the United States, France or India; have the highest crime rate, with just over three million people. Crimes against people, especially gays in Jamaica are being influenced through reggae music - the island is said to be a homophobic place, because of the people's attitude towards gay people.

Lastly, the marijuana problem in St Vincent and the Grenadines, which not as bad as the problem in Jamaica – personally I figure it is consequent to a more stable economy and strategic planning in St Vincent and the Grenadines.

St Vincent and the Grenadines is a multi-island nation in the Caribbean, located north of Grenada and South of St Lucia. St Vincent and the Grenadines is only one hundred and fifty square miles, with a population around one hundred and thirty thousand. The mainland has lush green mountains, which are blessed with rich volcanic soil; the ideal for marijuana harvesting.

Each year the Unites States Army would team up with members of the Special Services Unit on the island to eradicate drugs from the mountains. Often the Americans would stay for a couple of months, giving the farmers enough time to start a new farm. The local police force is not enough to execute the eradication process, although they are competent.

America does not always have the time to assist other countries with their problems. In this capacity, we need the presence of a regional force, which is committed to stay until the work is completed.

The islands are the ideal place to traffic drugs, because of the islands laid back environment and the little equipments, which are available. We hardly have the use of radar and helicopters to track and follow illegal drug activities. Nor do we have the manpower to eradicate the drug problem we are facing.

Additionally, there is another aspect of security in the region that I would like to touch on; security could be viewed as a multi-dimensional phenomenon. Security in the Caribbean is not only about protection against military threats, but has other dimensions, such as environmental, economical and political. Money laundering has been a major problem in the region where many companies and individuals have secretly hid their money and other assets. This is relatively easy in the region, because of particular factors, which exist – low taxation, bank secrecy and political instability amongst many more factors.

For the Caribbean to effectively combat money laundering we must enact laws that reveal the identity of the culprits, along with the correct training to identify and report these flaws to local law enforcements. In addition to this, financial assistance must to provided to adequately deal with these issues effectively and efficiently.

We all know the sanctions that the US place on us when we operate contrary to financial laws.

No single island in the region does possess adequate resources to combat this toxic problem. Thus, there is a need to combine our resources which will be adequate to fighting illegal drugs.

The United States is not committed to assist with our drug problem. This means that we have to fight this crime on our own. And make no mistake if one island is affected the other islands automatically are affected; not because we allowed it, but considering the closeness of the islands. This region unique in its own way; people in St Vincent and the Grenadines could sit in their front porch and see St Lucia across the Atlantic. The same could be said if you are sitting in your yard in northern parts of St Lucia watching over to Martinique in the north.

The United States, however, is assisting the Bahamas and Turks and Caicos in fighting their drug problem by introducing the Bahamas, America, Turks and Caicos – the BAT operation. This operation involves flying around on American choppers with a combination of Americans, Bahamas and Turks and Caicos law enforcements.

To me the only reason why the Americans have influenced to assist in this way is because of the countries' close proximity to their home. Grand Bahama, the Bahamas is just about thirty minutes in Bahamas Air and Providenciales in the Turks and Caicos Islands is an hour and fifteen minutes flying time on an American 747.

I am fearful that terrorism will soon spread its operations in the region. It is true that no major catastrophe relating to terrorism had occurred in the Caribbean; however, for me it is a matter of time.

Nowadays terrorist are seeking vulnerable places to strike. The recent bombings of the Marriot and Ritz Carlton hotels in Jakarta, Indonesia in July 2009 were the last place one would expect terrorist to strike. But the issue is not only terrorists coming to our region and strike, but the risk of our citizens converting to Islam and carry out terrorists' acts.

A couple of years back, a woman was beheaded in the bustling city of Kingstown, St Vincent and the Grenadines. I still wonder if this is the act of terrorism. However, it is true that many Iraqis beheaded some captured Americans during the second American-led invasion of Iraq.

It is good that some security systems in the region, particularly, in Trinidad and Tobago and Barbados are taking corrective measures to deal with this violent act. As the Director of Security at a large established hotel I am also being proactive in teaching how to combat terrorism.

The primary reason why a terrorist will target vulnerable places is because Americans are big targets for terrorists and it makes the job of the terrorist simpler when Americans are away from home and in vulnerable places like hotels in the Caribbean.

The American will do whatever it takes to bring justice for its citizens, therefore, we expect that if an act of terrorism is carried out on an American citizen while in the region, there is no doubt that the US will respond, whether diplomatically or militarily. However, trends indicate that the US is becoming weak economically and consequently it will become weak militarily. In this capacity, we must build our own regional security forces.

Also, many of our islands possess natural resources, which parts of the world require. Trinidad and Tobago has natural gas, which is being exported to other parts of the world outside of the Caribbean. Jamaica has bauxite, limestone and gypsum. Guyana is blessed with gold, bauxite, timber and shrimps. It is very easy for terrorist to claim these resources – let's say that they are in need and refuse to pay for them.

Furthermore, it won't be much longer before terrorism spreads its operation within our region. The big questions to ask here are, if terror strikes the Caribbean, is any single nation equipped to deal with this problem? And if not, are we going to wait on the US or other global armed forces for months before they respond? So where do we go from here?

In light of this, terrorism in the region is inevitable; it is just a matter of time before it strikes. Millions of American citizens visit our shores on a yearly basis and the trend shows that terrorists target Americans in unexpected places. We should not forget the hotel bombings in India and Indonesia, which targeted American citizens.

Global trends also indicate that countries are forming alliances and integrating their efforts in order to achieve shared responsibilities, shared resources, shared costs, and creating diversity in both their ideas and personnel. The European Union, the economic giant, has formed NATO, the intergovernmental military alliance, which constitutes a system of collective defence. The United States, another economic giant, has solicited the assistance of NATO and UN to fight the war of terror in Afghanistan.

It is safe to conclude that we need a regional force to police our nations -- land, sea and air. With the enormous drug trade, disasters, political unrests, peacekeeping missions, attempted coups d'état, other criminal activities and the advent of terrorism, the region must be prepared. We need a police force that would be readily available for deployment at any time and place. If a regional organization existed, Haiti would be a better place today. World leaders allowed Haiti's issues to escalate before they could intervene.

Should one of these acts occur, are we ready to deal with it?

I do not think!

Terrorism takes many forms, which makes it possible to exist in the Caribbean. There are also a number of reasons why terrorism could reach our shores.

It is obvious that the United States has its own agenda. We must understand that they are only assisting; it is something that they volunteer to do and not an obligation. The United Nations also assist the Caribbean from time to time.

If we want to be represented at the United Nations we must be one Caribbean.

According to trends the United States are mostly interested in places where they have interests.

There would come a time when our forces would have to operate outside the region boundaries, deployed in the best interest of the islands. It is quite obvious that many nations have fully equipped arm force with much capability to defend or initiate an offensive. If we initiate deployment then it is easier to get foreign forces to follow.

To establish such huge force, requires enormous time, finance and other resources, and include a lot of planning and negotiation through setting policy and procedures amongst other underlying challenges; therefore, we must communicate the change early enough and understand the benefits of the integration process. We could only make it happen if we unite our efforts and support the change. However, these factors should be the least of our concerns – we should get started with our new regional force.

I believe that adequate government spending is inevitable, but on the other hand it reduces cost collectively – it would reduce single state cost and set up in a way to promote education, health and sports. We would also have better deployment of arm forces throughout the region.

Through this entity our main goal will be to acquire regional cooperation in achieving peace, regional security and regional law, sustained human rights, economic stability and promote social progress.

I know that there are some risky commitments to this oneness such as negotiation about where and what the force would engage and negotiation in entering costly deployment – whether in the region or outside of the Caribbean.

One other problem I have identified with a regional system through security is that there might not be a security issue, which may encourage a regionalized solution, but after assessing the region, this challenge may never exist.

We have to build our own forces and stop our dependency on foreign arm forces that is decided to assist will respond in their own time and not when we needed them.

Security is everybody's business and every nation from Africa; to Europe, Asia and everyone else have their own arm forces except for us. We are not the "quiet" Caribbean anymore. Many factors have changed.

Hence, we need regional police to provide safety and security for all our citizens.

~ PART 5 ~

Politics

It has been more than twenty five years since the last nation in the Caribbean gained its independence from Europe, mainly from Britain, France and Spain. Haiti has gained its independence from France, Cuba and the Dominican Republic from Spain and the Eastern Caribbean, the Bahamas, Jamaica, Barbados and Trinidad and Tobago from Britain. Since then a number of countries have continued the British-type constitution, especially the English speaking Caribbean.

Moreover, a number of nations within the region are still dependent on Britain, France and the Netherlands and the United States.

This is one area where there is hardly any evidence of regionalism in the Caribbean. This is also one area where the Caribbean differs and strives to build on its own. In my opinion, too many people want power; therefore, it is hard to regionalize the political process.

There are many disputes amongst Caribbean islands, which must be fixed before regionalism can become a reality. A recent *bashment* between Barbados government and the government of St Vincent and the Grenadines had provoked days of headline news in the region. These differences were created from both countries blaming each other for the increases in drug use, mainly marijuana, and the shipment of this drug between these two countries. Barbados law enforcement has, over the past years, sentenced a number of Vincentians to many years in prison for the transshipment of illegal drugs to that island.

All of the dependent territories with the exception of Montserrat have always seen other Caribbean islands as invaders to their islands; often purporting that the citizens of the rest of the Caribbean islands are economically crippled. The same could be said about the Bahamas, Antigua and Barbuda, and Barbados to some extent.

In recent years, citizens in Trinidad and Tobago have been complaining about the constant rise in food and social commodities. According to news reports, the government of the twin republic state indicated that the government will have to effectively and efficiently manage the operations of the country. In addition, the Prime Minister at the time had encouraged the citizens to set future goals for themselves. There is a need for other Caribbean islands to take this initiative toward building their nations, but they must do so as a single unit; attempting to reach this goal as individual nations would only aggravate the situation.

Singly, the islands are not able to survive politically.

Presently the local government of the Turks and Caicos Islands, a British dependent country in the northern Caribbean, has been suspended the local Turks and Caicos Islands government pending further investigation into an alleged corruption scheme, and authorities from British assume leadership of the islands in the meantime.

In the meanwhile, the two local parties; the People Democratic Movement – PDM and the People National Party – PNP will battle for the office of government in the next general election when the opportunity does comes.

Most of the islands in the region, according to my assessment, are politically unstable. There are too many issues within our political systems. This range from parties fighting against parties to government making promises they can't fulfill. Some governments in the Caribbean are not committed to serving the citizens, hence, depleting their standards of living.

I must commend the governments of Barbados for placing enormous efforts in building their nation. This country has one of the highest standards in the region and to some extent in the world.

Barbados governments have always worked toward industrializing the country and provide political stability at home. It is true that Barbados to, have political disputes but it not to the extent as exist amongst other Caribbean nations.

Many time I dreamt about St Vincent and the Grenadines and for that matter the rest of the

Caribbean to secure a stable political system like the one, which existed in Barbados.

Although St Vincent and the Grenadines has a stable government for eighteen years under Sir James F. Mitchell and the New Democratic Party, I believe that political system in Barbados had not been matched.

I am also aware that most islands in the region constitutions vary somewhat, Cuba is in a bracket by itself; having transformed from a democratic state to a communist type constitution. Some of the islands used the British system, while other like the Dominican Republic and Haiti held unto the Spanish and French typed constitutions.

I must indicate that Communism although Communism never works it has its positive side. Let me highlight a few on them.

The first is that the citizens of the country that have adopted a Communist regime will not be encouraged to work, since they do not have the state provide all of their basic needs. However, under such rigid regime people are forced to work for the good of the entire state.

There are no distinguishing features in class. Everyone is on the same level. On one hand this might be a good feature, since it is highly impossible to suppress another person or group. This confirm the notion of equality; the equal distribution of goods and services to every citizens. But there are many other issues in society that Communism cannot eliminate.

Impressively, Communism allows all citizens to enjoy and have access to basic need, such as food, water, heath care, education, and includes all infrastructures – roads, bridges, railways and the likes. This takes away headaches, such as where the next meal will be coming from. There is no reason to worry since the state provides those basic amenities.

But ask yourself one question, can a single government provide all of the basic need its citizens? Let's take Cuba and its eleven million people into consideration, relative to the country's gross domestic product.

This theorem is highly criticized by most of the Western World, dominated by the United States. Sometimes I imagine what the world would be like if everyone is able to drive a BMW or an Escalade. I figured it would be chaos. There would not be enough roads to accommodate all the vehicles on a single island. This, however, is not the case of Communism. The state only provides the basic commodities, so where the other amenities do come from? Why provide some items and not all? The answer is that people have to fight for themselves if they want to live outside the perimeter of Communism.

The big problem in a Communist regime is that people are not motivated to work, since there is no real benefit. If people are being provided with the basics of life, why work? It is being provided whether you work or not.

This is only one problem among others.

In a Communist state there is not a single job that pays well for anyone to live a luxurious life style – a Communist state does not permit this. I know for a fact that the majority of West Indians would like to have luxurious commodities through hard work and not be confined to only possessing basic commodities.

I would also like to highlight some of the principles of Communism – these are traces of a Communist regime.

Foremost, is the act of a Marxist – Leninist doctrine of Communism, which proposes a defeat of Capitalism by revolution. The modern overthrowing of Capitalism is taking place in a slightly different way, where functioning democratic governments seek to switch from a capitalist market system to Communist market system through a vote of referendum, which does not clearly outline the facts of the given constitution. According to this theory, the end of morality absolutism and religion is encouraged. More so, after Communism is established the system is transferred into a totalitarian regime – controlling every aspect of the nation it was created for. This is the same system, which persecute people on demand. These activities are also evident in all nations that have practiced this political nightmare.

Also, there is the act of taking over the Transportation and Communication Departments. In addition, the government tends to take away private land ownership to state ownership. The government also would seize private owner ship of the Agriculture Sector and factories.

Similarly, the government would take full control over education and regional planning.

On the other hand there are some hideous downfalls of the Marxist system.

In a Communist regime there is no true government system set up. The people are not important and the leader does not need a vote to stay in power. In this capacity, the leader does everything he wants without consulting others under his command. Most of the people's right and freedom are taken away through rigid rules and regulations.

In light of this, the big question remains – how are we going to deal with Cuba's situation?

For me, the answer is simple. Personally, I disapprove of the notion of Communism. I can't imagine people living under a system where they are being deprived of vitality, sensitivity and intelligence. I am aware that the mixed system has it faults, but it is surrounds the people and what they wish to do – there is a sense of liberalism in countries that practice liberal democracy.

The fact that Cuba is a part of the West Indies and we should in no way exclude them – after all I am not trying to instill our norms and values into the lives of the Cuban people. I know that the people of that nation have the same sentiments like those of the rest of the Caribbean, but circumstances beyond their control have kept the people of Cuba in desperation for more than 40 years. They have no free movements, no human rights, no rights to property and many other features of a Communist regime. The people of Cuba did not vote for this painstaking psyche, it was forced on them by a leader who does not have a conscience and respect for human freedom.

The reason for their silence for so many years is because of oppression. They have no rights to speak out – remember it is not democracy. Every year hundred of Cubans are trying escape the hardship they face at home. One should thank the United States for its empathetic laws, which gave Cubans the right to stay in the US whether they entered legal or not; just an open minded resolution for the Cuban people.

We have to be careful of the Castro Raul's hard cores – civilian and military personnel who are loyal to Castro and his regime. These were the same people who went down to Grenada to facilitate the uprising there. This is an indication that the Cuban regime is trying to spread their ideologies within the smaller islands. The good thing about this attempted coup is that they failed to fully take over and established themselves.

Politics in Cuba is not the same as the wider Caribbean. The former present Fidel Castro has handed over power to his brother Raul Castro; it seemed as though politics in that country has become a family business.

Much recognition should be extended to the United States that defused the Cuban's attempt to remove democracy from that tiny Caribbean state; Communism was too close to home.

Currently, all eyes are on a few smaller Caribbean Islands especially St Vincent and the Grenadines, with big influence from Venezuela. Recently, Hugo Chavez has been visiting St Vincent and the Grenadines regularly. In fact, report out of St Vincent and the Grenadines and the popular media stated that Venezuela's soldiers were invited guests of that island's Independence Day parade – the latest being October 27, 2009.

Reports out of St Vincent and the Grenadines indicate that President Hugo Chavez is playing a major role in the decision making of the state; ranging from the kind of projects being undertaken by the state to the country's fiscal policy.

There is skepticism that Prime Minister of St Vincent and the Grenadines wants to implement and practice Socialism. Many talks would suggest that this true. Lately, the government wanted to change the constitution when the prime minister begged the Vincentian public to vote for the new constitution through a referendum, on which most citizens voted, no. I would like to discuss this direction for a moment and this is in no way contrary to what I mentioned earlier.

The constitutional change in St Vincent and the Grenadines, or for that matter in any other parts of the Caribbean, is needed. If the constitution is being used to remove the British as head of state then all Vincentians should be ready for such change. The British are in no way assisting the islands; therefore, they are of no use to us. The Republic of Trinidad and Tobago and Dominica have gone through this process and they remained democratic nations.

Conversely, I am against the new constitution if it is a trick into changing the political system from being democratic into a Socialist regime.

Moreover, the Prime Minister of St Vincent and the Grenadines have been mingling with some world leader who are associated with Socialism, Communism, or Totalitarianism; the Iranian President, Cuban President and the President of Venezuela. Many people are questioning the motives behind these associations.

Press releases confirmed that the governments of these three non-democratic nations are assisting St Vincent and the Grenadines with the New International airport, which to date cost more than US two hundred million dollars - more than four hundred million Eastern Caribbean dollars.

If this is true then St Vincent and the Grenadines is on the right path, hoping that there is not a catch to this generosity.

Everyone would realize that the US government is closely monitoring the activities of the government of St Vincent and the Grenadines, however, the fact remains that our nations have not been given the assistant needed to enhance the quality of life and; therefore, it is in the interest of the governments of the region to seek alternatives.

Cuba must not be eliminated from certain aspect of the region's quest for regionalism – security, agriculture and other aspect of the economy. It would be a risk to link Cuban soldiers with the rest of the regions; Cuba being a Communist states and the most populous nation in the West Indies.

I believe in a regional committee in an effort to negotiate change of political system in Cuba. Maybe a Caribbean presence would make a difference rather than a US presence that everyone identifies as a bully. As a contingency plan we should go ahead and develop our regional police force to deal with Cuba, militarily – a last resort effort to remove the Communist regime there.

Our neighbors in Cuba are suffering. They do not want this type of government; therefore it's our obligation to fight in an effort to liberate them.

The Cubans are afraid to speak out – being afraid of oppression; hence, collectively, we must do the talking and assist them in any way we can.

Most people and states, including the US dislike the idea of Communism for the same reason that it is a failed political system; one of the reasons being that it is a system that is forced upon the people.

The other parts of the Caribbean - the Eastern Caribbean are mainly governed by a Westminster type parliament – the British democratic system. However, there are some variations in the Dominican Republic, the Netherland Antilles, and Haiti, Martinique and Guadeloupe.

The entire Eastern Caribbean has a democratic political government where power is granted to the Prime Minister through an election. In our societies, all citizens are equal and have access to the same level of power – where citizens are promised certain levels of freedom and liberties.

What I admired about the term democracy is the virtual rights to vote. Unlike the Communist system, citizens here have the right to vote for who they want to rule and represent them. In a democratic society if the people are not satisfied with the status quo they have a right to remove the present government through an election. Conversely, in a communist state, citizens have to accept what is being handed down to them. In most cases the people are not permitted to talk and feared being tortured and imprisoned - a system contrary to liberal democracy.

One thing I would like to see introduced in the planning process of the democratic movement is the involvement of the private sector. We might argue that the government was elected to do all the planning, but in essence, the government is an elected few who does not know every aspect of the community market, and their needs. The truth is this sector is part of the system, they are at risk and they should be able to assist the government in planning, which include standardizing price of goods and services. The other fact is that the private sector might be experiencing problems relating to real growth, therefore, a change in price for goods and services might have to set at a different rate to acquire required rate of return.

On a personal note, I dislike the way politics are being conducted in the Caribbean and for that matter around the world. I must highlight it is more professional in countries like the United States, Canada and England. Although there governments are practically stable. Particularly, I do not endorse the political process and environment in St Vincent and the Grenadines and the wider Caribbean. I have witnessed a few electoral campaigns where candidates practically and consistently demoralized their opponents; rather than outlining their plans for the forward moving of the country. What I am recommending is that the leaders discuss the issues affecting the countries in an effort to find solution to fit them.

Too often political rivals discuss each other personal business instead of telling the people what they will do for them and how they would achieve results.

Politics in the Caribbean create a hateful and unprofessional environment, which should not be the case. The political leaders tend to set up fights between party supporters.

I know politics creates a similar environment throughout the region; therefore, I am employing a focus on the pressing issues, such as the economical, social, and environmental, amongst other issues.

There is a popular phrase about politicians in the St Vincent and the Grenadines, which states that "All politicians are the same." They promise many things during the campaigning process and once the election process has concluded, the leaders disappeared; sometimes with millions of tax payers' dollars.

One shouldn't wonder why there are party clashes in these parts of the world. The leaders are the ones who are virtually responsible for the hate that people develop for each other, because of their election choices.

It is a custom that the streets are filled with people carrying flyers, "T"-shirts and chanting as political leaders deliberate; the media will announce and display their executive expressions of human immaturity while the communities, towns and villages alienate themselves from each other's opinions and ideologies; the political war without bloodshed. This is the exact environment as St Vincent and the Grenadines (SVG) and other nations gear for their next general election.

During electoral campaigns the media, politicians and citizens alike display their immaturity toward each other's ideologies. Quiet parishes with imaginary borders become hostile territories guarded by political jurisdictions and insurgents. The media carefully promotes its favorite parties while politically demising and demoralizing their opponents.

It is imperative that people understand that it is the right of other to follow and support whatever party they wish. During electoral campaigns politician are too manipulative and one has to be very assertive.

Conversely, other Caribbean countries have slightly different political systems. Puerto Rico is a bit different as it is a governed republican state, has three branch government; a legislative, executive and senate. The current head of state is Barrack Obama, the President of the United States of America.

In addition to this, the US Virgin Islands – St John, St Croix and St Thomas, each has an unincorporated organized territory of the United States. Citizens of the US Virgin Islands are deemed US citizens; however, they are not allowed to vote in US general elections.

Puerto Rico and the United States Virgin Islands are in very good shape politically, since their territories and governments are regulated by the United States Congress. The first time I went to Puerto Rico I thought the pilots had made a mistake and landed somewhere in the United States, because of the country's infrastructure, which closely resembles that of the United States; however, there is federal government that is elected to oversee the island's daily operations; social, political and economical.

Politically, Puerto Rico is said to be stable with only a few disagreement to some US decisions. In light of this, the relationship between Puerto Rico and the United States is a continuous debate; I sense that Puerto Ricans want to become an independent nation – forming a government that would allow them to be fully in charge of the entire commonwealth's operations and decision making. I also have the feelings that the people of the Commonwealth of Puerto Rico wants to represent themselves in all international conferences, such as the United Nations.

It must be noted that Puerto Ricans have the privilege to live and work in the United States. They also are termed as United States citizens whether they were born in Puerto Rico or on the US mainland. Despite this freedom, the people of the Puerto Rico are desperately seeking to be an independent nation.

We often asked if this is the right move when regionalism is not a true phenomenon amongst Caribbean Islands.

There is a similar situation in the United States Virgin Islands.

In fact the Netherland Antilles of the West Indies Aruba, Curacao and Bonaire, and St Maarten, St Eustatius and Saba have a slightly different government where they have a governor and a Prime minister, the governor being the head of State. However, these islands have their local government that takes care of local operations and they are governed by an executive branch and a legislative branch. Although, these Islands are constitutional monarchy of the Netherlands, they are not a part of the European Union. This is a big difference relative to Puerto Rico and the US Virgin Islands and their constitutional rights in the United States.

There are mixed representations within the Netherlands Antilles. Aruba has chosen an autonomous country status within the Kingdom of the Netherlands, and to date Curacao and St Maarten are seeking this same status. The other islands in the Netherlands Antilles are also seeking closer relationship with the Netherlands.

The Netherland Antilles like any other overseas territory have their own local governments that would undertake local interest and assist each other when the need arises. In this sense, the Netherlands Antilles are governed by an elected unicameral parliament consists of twenty people. There is prime minister and a governor who would serve for six years at a time. The governor is in charge of the islands under the direction of the authorities in the Netherlands.

Similarly, Martinique and Guadeloupe are two overseas departments of France with full political and legal rights. They are French citizens and form part of the European Union. Similarly, Martinique and Guadeloupe political system carries almost the same process of those overseas territories with a unicameral General Council that take care of it their local interests, While they report to authorities in France.

St Martin and St Barthelemy are also similar. These small Caribbean Islands are overseas collectivity of France that recently seceded from Guadeloupe. These islands are part of the European Union and reports back to France.

These political systems came about consequent to drastic political changes made by France immediately after World War II.

At the time, Guadeloupe and Martinique were governed by governor from France. These governors oversee the countries operations - law enforcement, public services and governmental operations. Thereafter, the citizens of Martinique were not satisfied with the autonomy, thus, they rioted for more control over control over legislations and expenditures.

However, despite this set back on the part of France, the French government assisted these oversees departments with a higher quality of life.

Interestingly, these islands political systems are formerly democratized and stable.

Trends around the world show that Communist states have failed miserably. Firstly, most citizen do not endorse act of Communism. There is no way a single government is able to provide all the basic needs for all its citizens, especially countries with huge population. The problem begins when economic challenges surfaced and there is not a contingency plan. Additionally, many nations around the world do not support this Marxist theory.

In my mind I cannot recall any nation that actually voted Communism. As a matter of fact, Communism only exists under a revolutionary fervor.

I cannot end this part without reflecting on Communist Cuba.

In an effort to involve the Communist state in the regional process let's showcase our very own, the Republic of Cuba. I figured that one of the main reasons why Cuba had failed is because of the US embargo to that island. Personally, I don't believe in embargos, since millions of people living under a Communist regime, go hungry on a daily basis. In this sense, the America government needs to lift the embargo on these Communist states. Let me just mention that millions of people in North Korea go hungry each day under a similar and rigid regime. I would prefer to see America invade Cuba rather than the economic turmoil that its people are facing today.

I strongly believe that lifting the embargo would hamper the revolutionary regime, which Castro had built. Castro as smart as he is, had over the years, blamed the failure of his Communist state on America's embargo. Lifting the embargo would show the true facts about the country's economic failure - the inflicted Castro Raul regime.

Fortunately, if the embargo is lifted then more Americans will travel largely to the island, therefore, trade and culture is exchanged. In this is capacity,

Cubans would want to adopt part of the American culture and to be part of commerce, hence those people who were living under bondage for so long could eventually distance themselves from Castro Socialist ideas.

I am in favor of the Unites States President, Barack Obama's vision to Communist states. He said in his pre-election campaign that he would encourage talks with leaders of these nations, without pre-conditions. I see this as the way forward for any forward-looking nation. Everyone blames the US for their failure. Considering these accusations the US President should sit down with leader of Communist nations regardless of the status quo. This will show the world that America is willing to talk to the enemy and listen to their complaints and try to assist.

Interestingly, Cuba does trade with other countries around the globe including Latin and South America, Europe and Canada

Everyone knows Cuba could not survive without the assistance of the Soviet Union. When the Soviet Union could not assist Cuba as before, especially during the economic downturn of the Soviet Union Cubans began to experience economic downturn, because the state could no longer provide for its people. There were no money to pay for goods and services and to maintain facilities, hence, Cuban Industries collapsed, and there were no proper health care for the citizens considering the well-trained doctors in Cuba.

Castro had to turn to Capitalism so he could feed the people of Cuba. He opened up the shores of his country to outsiders and legalized the United States dollar – he opened Cuba's doors, so just enough cash could come in.

Fidel Castro is not dumb leader, he actually acquire a law degree at Havana University. He turned to Capitalism in order to save his rigid Socialistic regime. Many people are pondering why the Cuban leader never gave up on the old regime, which failed for more than four decades. The answer lies in his hardcore loyalists to Marxist Leninist theory and he refused to let go of power; henceforth, he failed distribute this power to better equip the country's economic condition and the people's standard of living; an intelligent and influential leader with conceited and dogmatic personalities.

Although Castro opened up the doors of one of the most beautiful islands in the Caribbean the leader was careful not to let it spread wider than he had wanted. A number of goods from the United States and other parts of the globe were, in small amounts, available to the Cuban people. This was a new era in the lives of the Cuban citizens – a phenomenon that is new to the people of that country.

Russia, a great country during the cold war had also fallen, because of its Socialist ideologies. Once a superpower and still is, but is has fallen to a point where it is vulnerable to some superpowers like the United States and England in terms of military response. It depleted economic environment has placed the country in a worsening global position.

With similar features of Cuba, Russia had focus too much on inventing military capabilities – an effort to obtain a defensive position against the world's biggest superpower, the United States and its ally the United Kingdom.

Just to mention the People's Republic China had remained unpopular relative to its Socialist and Communist type rule. However, the country has risen economically. I believe the reason for the upbeat in the economy of the Communist state is the fact that the country is changing its government system. Some aspects of the country are liberal while other aspects are still under an authoritarian rule, along with the country's ability to innovate and the fact that cheap labor exists in China. The People's Republic of China has one of the most brutal histories of human rights violation. This suggests that this country's political system is following Communist ideologies while other aspects - economic lean more toward a liberal democratic system.

If china had not changed it economic system the country would not prosper and it is perceived that this Communist state would end up like much of the other countries that practice Communism and Socialism. The fact that China is one of United States biggest trader, has positioned that country's economy as one of the largest economies in the world and the fastest global economy.

It is evident that Socialism and Communism ideologies have failed around the world. It would be a lack vision and accession for those leaders who would either want to instill these political nightmares or keep them.

Regionalizing the Caribbean through politics is one of our ultimate goals. I believe that the challenge ahead of us is a difficult one; although most of our islands are governed under the democratic system. As much, most of the effort should be directed toward the Republic of Cuba and its Communist regime - and getting rid of the family politics that exist there.

The Caribbean has to keep its individual government that would undertake its local operations. Furthermore, the regions have to create some form of committee or council to deal with regional issues and in this sense, there is a need to employ a third party; a system that as no formal or personal alignment with the region. This effort would ensure that focus is not centralized, but attributed evenly.

It is natural that there will be many controversies relating to what areas of the region to focus political realm.

Moreover, there is a need for that political committee or council to focus on those affairs of the region in an effort to strengthen the political power and governing bodies, manufacture efficiencies of scale and encourage decentralization – dispersing decision making with the approval of the people.

In this capacity, the Caribbean should institute a West Indian Cabinet with the sole responsibility for enacting and initiating legislation and making decision on a daily basis. Also, its sole responsibility is to serve the entire region and its member states. Ideally, this cabinet would consist of one member from each member state. A suggested time in office for the president of this cabinet should be about four years and a president from one of our islands. It is also recommended that this president be elected by the regional parliament and not by individual islands.

An election by individual islands would certainly create national bias. For example, Cuba is the most populous island in the region and it is obvious that Cuban will vote for Cubans, therefore, it is possible that a Cuban will always be elected as president. Conversely a small state, such St Vincent and the Grenadines would also want to vote for a Vincentian national, but considering the size of that state, there is no chance of having a president being elected from that country; therefore, this type of election is not encourage - the president of the Caribbean should be elected on merit, not popularity.

To add, this body should also have a judicial branch inherent of the Caribbean Court of Justice – Magistrates, Supreme and Appeal courts with a clear objective to ensure the laws of the region are confirmed and interpreted according to treaties. The purpose of the courts is to critically evaluate the legal aspects of the conduct of the West Indian institutions. This is enacted to ensure that each nation adhere to legality of the treaties.

The Magistrates court is consist of one Magistrate a prosecutor and defense lawyers and it is assigned to interpret Caribbean law and to guarantee that the law is being interpreted to all members of the region through a summary, criminal and civil procedures.

Similarly, the Supreme Court is the next high court in the Caribbean and it is the highest judicial court. Cases heard in the Supreme Court are first heard before a magistrate. This court consists of a judge and jury. The Supreme Court mainly hears offences criminal nature.

One tradition that bothers me is the use of a jury in a supreme court. Generally, jurors are citizens who have clean record, often those who hold some form of class in society. These people do not know law and it is true that most of them are not able to interpret the laws set out before them. Furthermore, these individuals do not know the points to prove in deciding whether there is or is not enough evidence to convict a particular person. It often wound up in wrongful imprisonment of individuals especially if the accused person is an outsider to that particular jurisdiction. Therefore, it is ninety nine percent of the time, that that outsider will be convicted by the jury for a crime he or she might not be associated with. Hence, I do not believe in jury; a judge is all that is needed in a court of law to determine whether someone is guilty or not.

The Appeal court also hears criminal offenses from sentencing resulting from the Supreme Court. It normally consists of three judges, defense lawyers and a prosecutor. Each judge listened to verbal argument of the case and makes a decision.

The Eastern Caribbean has initiated the move of integrating our judicial system by introducing the Eastern Caribbean Supreme Court. This court has jurisdiction within the entire Eastern Caribbean including the British Virgin Islands, Anguilla and Montserrat.

The Caribbean must enact a legal system; hence, the principal legal system should be in the form of three binding instruments.

The first being a legislative act, which should be in effect throughout the member states as law, occurring or operating at the same time.

The other should be the legislative act, which demands the entire nation to obtain some form of results without directing what the results should be. In fact, this legislative act allows member states the freedom to choose whatever rules they want to enact.

The last being right be make decisions by member states. Some decisions making to be made by member states include manufacturing issues and prices for goods and services.

This legal system must be established and its purpose is to enact legislations to affect the entire region and its citizens. This Caribbean law should be enacted in a way to ignore conflicting laws of the islands of the region, so that the Caribbean law could take effect.

Ideally, a number of treaties would have to be developed and sign concerning the various aspects of regionalism amongst nations to carry out Caribbean law in individual states.

Furthermore, I endorse the notion of a standardized Caribbean passport. This is a move, which would encourage our quest for regionalizing the Caribbean. It is a freshness of breathe to see all the Caribbean nations wave their Caribbean Community passports. It allows us to remove all the individual barriers, which often separates us. This environment is cleaner and more appreciative by the majority of Caribbean nationals.

This was not so in recent times when we all have our individual passports. There were many disputes about whose passport has the best color; the right size and the most unique design. We competed against each other in a simple document called a passport. Nowadays, that has changed, except that the free movement of good and service and citizens have yet to materialize.

I also want to stress the idea for one flag. I believe we have already adapted that ideology – the West Indies cricket team flag. To my knowledge, this flag is only hoisted when the regional cricket team is in action. There is an urgent need to raise this regional flag at every government headquarters throughout the region.

This flag has to be flown when our push for regionalism has been achieved; therefore, we must hoist this flag at every regional and international function; at home and abroad, whether it is through sports, tourism, politics, environment, economics and the likes.

There is no doubt that our political arena has to be adjusted to allow us to represent the Caribbean among the rest of the world. We should be sending representatives to the United Nations conferences, G8 summits and the Geneva Conventions.

I foresee many years of painstaking planning and researching. I also identified conflicts between many nations and the act of secession; considering the "Big island" "Small island" connotations, which exist within the Caribbean.

There has been enormous conflicts between "Small islands" and "Big islands." Citizens from the larger islands have always envisioned the citizens of the smaller islands to be weaker in all aspects. The problem always comes from the countries that labeled themselves as the More Develop Countries – mostly Jamaica, and Barbados, and Trinidad and Tobago to some extent. To my knowledge Trinidad and Tobago has been involved in many activities of the forward movement of the region.

Recently, Barbados' Prime Minister Hon David Thompson warned that there were going to be changes in that country's immigration policy and practice; giving preference to Barbadian nationals relative to employment – a direction contrary to the Caribbean

Community – CARICOM treaty. This effort would stifle the free movement of educated Caribbean nationals and the vision to integrate the region politically.

Consequently, this issue has created dialogues between the Prime Minister of Barbados, David Thompson and Guyana's President Bharrat Jagdeo, and St Vincent and the Grenadines' Prime Minister Dr. Ralph Gonsalves.

I vision this as a long lasting problem for the CARICOM nations from Barbados. It is obvious that Barbados would stall the move forward to closer integration. This country's economy has been one of the top economies amongst Caribbean Islands, hence, the country high employment rates. No question why so many other Caribbean nationals flocked the shores of Barbados seeking employments.

I suggest that country's that failed to cooperate should be left out the equation and promote the movement with those countries that are in line.

As I reflect, many Caribbean Islands disagreed on fundamental political issues in the region, hence, the challenges ahead of us. Many problems arise from ocean boundaries. Turks and Caicos Islands and the Dominican Republic have issues over ocean banks - some area in the Atlantic Ocean between the two countries; disagreeing on how far on the banks fishermen could fish. This is only one issue that exists in the region and this should in no way discourage our leaders from going forward on political issues, which affects the Caribbean and they must seek ways to regionalize this Caribbean effort.

The heads of government of the Eastern Caribbean are always the ones to initiate the vision, which holds that the Caribbean should and could be one. These leaders have, for many decades ago, visioned that regionalism is the direction in which the Caribbean should be heading. I believe that the Eastern Caribbean had this vision for oneness before the European Union. Evidently, the leaders of the European Union have use regionalism and have gained much progress in this capacity; making them a continent to recon with.

Ideally, enhancing the political powers of the governing bodies in the region from an individual state to a larger system could gain economies of scale, distribute the resources of the region in a meaningful way, which would benefit the entire region, position the region on the competitive stage and dispersing the decision making process in light of what the people want.

Hitherto, there is an urgent need to negotiate common foreign policy cooperation amongst the Caribbean states in an effort to work together on international trade, through the existence of a Caribbean Political Cooperation.

We must establish treaties with the goal of developing the interest of the Caribbean Community and the entire international community, which involve supremacy law, democracy and human rights. The realized benefit of such warranting criteria of regionalism in the Caribbean is to sustain the economic and political environment of each member states that wants to execute admittance standards of the Caribbean integration process. This phenomenon could create a positive impact on countries like Cuba that might want to remove its Communist regime and adopt a democratic style leadership.

Regionalizing the political arena can create many problems including complete separation from the entire regional political system especially in situations where cultural differences are present. This issue should not be ruled out but I doubt that it will create much of a problem, since most of the region's cultures coincide; even the Dominican Republic and Cuba, Haiti, Martinique and Guadeloupe and to some extent Curacao, Bonaire and Aruba that have Spanish, French and Dutch associated nations. There are many factors within our culture where we can be identified collectively. Don't forget that our islands were once ruled by the British, French, or some other European Country and in some cases a combination of two or more European powers.

I do not believe that the Eastern Caribbean States would be a problem, as we have initiated this process a long time ago and are awaiting the compromise of the other Caribbean nations, mainly the More Developed Countries, Jamaica, Trinidad and Tobago, Guyana and Barbados.

Personally, I do not like the idea of politics as there is no honesty involved. Politicians say and do anything to gain power - therefore, citizens are manipulated into voting for them. However, I am forced to get involved in politics for the sole reason that I want to pursue regionalism in the region. The first step is to sell my philosophical ideologies through this book and, thereafter, run for government in St Vincent and the Grenadines.

It is a very urgent need to change the way we run our political system and the only way I believe I could make a difference is to run for the office of the Prime Minister in St Vincent and the Grenadines – giving me enough power to move forward on this idea.

Too many Caribbean governments have been watchdogs. Many leaders have been accused of mingling with tax payers' money and leave the citizens to suffer. Reports from around the world indicated that there were corruptions in several Caribbean Islands.

I would like to see government working for people and not for a selective few.

In fact, the Caribbean had togetherness decades ago during our grand parents' era. In this era, other Caribbean nationals run for office in other islands without any questions asked. John Crompton, St Lucia's Prime Minister is a Vincentian that migrated to St Lucia. Edward Seaga that was the Jamaica's Prime Minister born in Boston Massachusetts to Jamaican parents, and Maurice Bishops who was Prime Minister of the People's Revolutionary Government of Grenada.

Although Maurice Bishop was a Grenadian politician, he was born in Aruba, Netherlands Antilles.

Nowadays, one West Indian cannot even speak about issues affecting other Caribbean nations. Recently, the Prime Minister of St Vincent and the Grenadines went to Jamaica and raised some political issues, which ignited friction between the prime minister and the people of Jamaica.

Our current political system does not allow for other nation to intervene in other nations' affairs.

How could this oneness be promoted with so many regional barriers?

In the meanwhile, through this book, I am employing all leaders throughout the Caribbean; whether they are French, English, Creole, Patois, Spanish or Dutch, to start the process.

A good way to start is to set up a committee or council that would plan around these ideologies.

Let's put our difference aside and build the ultimate team, which would give the rest of the world a run for their money.

With your cooperation the Caribbean region can become one of the world's political power houses.

Each state and province has its own local government – mayors, governors and senate yet controlled by the Federal Government - the president. The European Union has implemented a paradigm that the region could fashion.

~ PART 6 ~

Culture

Cultural issues within the Caribbean have been leveled to a minimum for many decades. This is consequent to the fact that most Caribbean islands, especially the Eastern Caribbean, Barbados and Trinidad and Tobago are quite similar, identity and shared ideologies.

Many of the norms and rituals in the regions have similar features, where we all can be identified. This is a good way forward, since we share similar ideas and thoughts. Just to name a few, around the Caribbean we "Pitch marbles," worship our God in similar manner, we celebrate Christmas each year just about the same.

Our cultures describes the ways in which citizens throughout the region express themselves in an effort to form groups, define identity and unity amongst other groups, and sometime identify themselves in unique ways.

In the region there are some major differences among us, particularly the other countries that speak different languages. Furthermore, there are slight differences amongst some of our islands that derived from the same cultural background.

Let me highlight some of the many differences we have. This is true when comparing Jamaica to the Eastern Caribbean. There music is different from that of the Eastern Caribbean, the way they pronounced and say certain words also vary; the Jamaicans tend to remove the letter "H" from words and placed the same letter in words where it is not needed.

Traveling to other parts of the Caribbean does not create problems in terms of knowing what and how to do things.

After traveling to many other Caribbean islands and living between other Caribbean nationals I perceive a great similarity in our culture and moreover many differences, yet unique.

The reason for my claim being that some of the things we do and say are similar and in many cases it is the same.

It is not a coincidence that we have many similarities within our cultures. Dating back to the days of the Slave Trade between Africa to the Caribbean by the Europeans, the Caribbean became similar. First each island had their native people the Carib Indians and then the Awarak tribes. We all know that the Europeans had killed the entire native population from all of the islands except for Dominica and St Vincent and the Grenadines where a small fraction of these people still exist.

The Caribs, in those days, survived through hunting and fishing. Most of the islands have fertile soils, which is important to agriculture. In addition, the entire island chain is surrounded by sea and ocean, making it the ideal place for fishermen. The foods of choice back then were maize what we called corn today, cassava and fish. This is still a tradition amongst many Caribbean Islands, including the Spanish settlements of Cuba and the Dominican Republic.

The Caribbean is home to thousands of farmers and fishermen. As a matter of fact, in St Vincent and the Grenadines the local population celebrate

Fisherman's Day and it is one of the many holidays there. They also have a National Farmers Movement, which attend to the affairs of the hundreds of farmers living on that island.

Dominica and St Vincent and the Grenadines still have the "Carib dance" a dance, which existed amongst the Carib people before Christopher Columbus rediscovery of the islands.

The Carib that exist in Dominica still live primitively - they settled in areas remote from the rest of the island's population and live the traditional way where hunting and fishing is the key to survival.

A similar way of living existed amongst the Carib people in St Vincent and the Grenadines up until about twenty years ago when these people started to mingle with the rest of the population in St Vincent and the Grenadines.

Through sports the Caribs were able to associate themselves with the other isolated demographics. Education today, also play a big role in the lives of the Caribs people, some of whom are holding ministerial offices in St Vincent and the Grenadines. Interestingly, they have withdrawn themselves from their indigenous communities and seek residence amongst other residents, especially in communities closed to the city of Kingstown.

Many years ago these people live in a remote area in the northern part of mainland St Vincent where no electricity existed and grass huts still being used as houses. Today, this primitive outlook has changed where grass huts turned into brick and concrete houses; some small; some medium size and some large mansions.

On the other hand the cultures of the Caribbean stems from Carib culture and many heritages including European and most evidently the African heritage.

The European heritage is evident through the many ethnic groups exist within our islands and also the shared architecture of our towns and cities. Cities and towns within the eastern Caribbean, Dominican Republic, Haiti Martinique and the Netherland Antilles share similar architecture, which stems from colonial times. Most of our buildings are long and narrow, just a few stories high, designed with arches and the pathways paved with cobblestones. No question why St Vincent and the Grenadines' capital is better known as the city of arches.

In the Caribbean Antigua and Barbuda, and Barbados still retained most of the British Colonial past. The Dominican Republic and Cuba still hold Spanish monuments and Puerto Rico to some extent that possess modern American architecture and other major American rituals. Aruba also seemed Dutch sustained some Dutch influence and Martinique, Guadeloupe and Haiti are smaller fraction of France and its values.

What struck me are the cultural aspects, which exists largely among the islands of the Eastern Caribbean. These islands are so similar and you almost cannot tell our nationalities. Because of the islands' rich volcanic contents, the British and French soldiers battled for the islands for decades, as they were ideal for agricultural purposes. This is the same reason for the mixture of British and French norms and values. However, Barbados is the only island in the Caribbean, which was never occupied by another European country – having been occupied only by the British. I believe the reason for this is that the island's soil contents are ideal and agriculture friendly.

Most of the islands are English speaking while the remaining few speak French Creole and Spanish.

In St Lucia and Dominica the people speak both English and Creole. In Antigua and Barbuda, St Vincent and the Grenadines, Montserrat, St Kitts, Grenada, British and US Virgin Islands, the Cayman Islands and Anguilla have similar accents – English combined with French patois. In fact, Jamaica speaks in a similar way. To some extend St Lucia and Dominica also express themselves in that manner. Most of the Eastern Caribbean still have many French and English surnames, towns and cities.

Puerto Rico has some distinct feature of speaking both English and Spanish. The Spanish speaking features are derived from the Spanish settlements on that island and the English was influence by its association to the United States.

St Lucia and Dominica are also distinct, since these nations speak English and a French Creole, which is largely spoken in the rural areas of these two islands. This bilingualism is a result of history - the British and French constant fighting for the islands where governance was changed a few times during those periods of wars.

Some islands have a wide variety of languages spoken by immigrants to those islands, which is not influenced by history. In the Turks and Caicos Islands a vast population speaks French Creole and Spanish, by immigrations who settled the islands from Haiti and the Dominican Republic, in search for better life - the Turks and Caicos Islands being an English speaking Country.

Our African heritage is also an outstanding one, as most of the people living in the Caribbean are from African descent. Evidently, most of African culture and customs occupied the lives of the islanders and this is no different in the Spanish and French speaking nations, through arts, dancing, religious ceremonies and our thoughts. Being a native of St Vincent and the Grenadines, I often identify myself to a Haitian national through dance and arts. The presence of Africa in the Caribbean has influence Voodoo across Caribbean nations, which is more wide spread in Haiti; Rastafarianism in the islands and mostly practiced in Jamaica; and the limbo dancing with is practice on similar levels throughout the Eastern Caribbean.

Furthermore, the Caribbean way of life is certainly a typical tropical influence. Undoubtedly, our music, Language, attitudes and beliefs, religions and more are shaped by the topography and climate of our region – hence expressing our colonial pasts.

Not withholding the East Indians who have contributed meaningfully within the islands and have also retained some of their cultural practices – making the culture of the islands a unique practice on a global level. At least, this is one aspect of our quest for regionalism, which can position us on top of the world stage.

Some of the differences, which exist mainly derived from the other countries such as the Dominican Republic, Puerto Rico and Cuba, Haiti, Martinique, Guadeloupe, that have Spanish and French values. Bonaire, Curacao, Aruba and Aruba that possess norms from the Netherland Antilles and some English speaking Caribbean countries like the Bahamas and Turks and Caicos that have mostly influence by American way of life.

The Bahamas and Turks and Caicos have different accents from the rest of the Caribbean. Also, Barbados and Trinidad and Tobago possess a slightly different accent from the rest of the Caribbean; Barbados being influenced by Britain and Trinidad and Tobago by Spanish legacy.

From a regional prospective, the Eastern Caribbean, Trinidad and Tobago, Barbados, even Martinique, Guadeloupe and Haiti cannot be identified with the type of dance displayed in the Dominican Republic; amongst many other cultural factors.

Therefore, there are many major aspects of our culture, which makes us similar or different.

Our music and dances varies somewhat and while each island is separating themselves trying to create the most influential music and dances, thereby, developing modern music – a combination of two or more type of music to create a modern kind of music. Some of this music is culturally oriented by past colonial status. This, however, is not so bad, since it create modernity in the region, and highlight artiste from different kinds of music throughout the islands.

Soca and reggae artiste have bind their music together and create ragga-soca.

Unconsciously, the islands have integrated in this unique phenomenon.

The Eastern Caribbean is a lover of calypso and soca and identifies reggae as part of their culture, since it originated from another Caribbean Island. Arguably, these types of music has originally established in Trinidad and Tobago, where the Lord Shorty was born and displayed his musical talent for decades. Other big names in the Caribbean include the Mighty Sparrow, Becket Alston Cyrus, Red Plastic Bag, Lord Kitchener,

Byron Lee and thee Dragonaires, David Rudder and many more.

Soca originated from calypso music and there is a slight difference between the two. Calypso, as seen in St Vincent and the Grenadines is a more conscious rhythm, which mostly highlight the political arena within ones country. Soca on the other hand is a more dancehall upbeat form of music.

Our modern day calypso and soca artistes like Rupee, Machel Montano, Kevin Lyttle and Jamesy P have enticed the American and European public.

Pan music has also originated out of the twin island republic of Trinidad and Tobago and has widely spread across the region. To date, I still do not understand steel pan and how it is made. Steel pan makers carve out a fifty five gallon drums into a musical sensation – it is pure genius on part of the Trinidadian; a skill that was candidly handed down to citizens across the Caribbean. Many respect to the pannists who learned these notes and attract thousands of people around the world.

Again, I believe that this was a direction in which we should go if we want to regionalize our nations. One country introduced and the others support.

But within calypso and soca music there are many other modern songs which are unique to each island. Let me name a few.

In Trinidad and Tobago there is Chutney-soca and parang; In St Vincent and the Grenadines are chutney and string band music; and in Barbados ringband and tuk.

Another major type of music in the region is the Raggae music, which was developed in Jamaica. Few other Caribbean islands have adopted this style of music; however, the other islands listen to this kind of music on a large scale. Conversely, not much Jamaicans have excelled or even vent calypso and soca. Byron Lee and the Dragonaires are Jamaicans who have made it in the spotlight. The irony is he migrated to Trinidad and Tobago where his made is soca debut.

Most Jamaicans do not like calypso and soca because they believe that reggae is the best music the world has listened to. I have heard many arguments surrounding how low-down calypso and soca music are and how unwelcome this type of music is in Jamaica. There is no more explanation needed to the reason why hardly any calypso and soca artiste come out from Jamaica.

The lesson here is that individual nations rank the different components of their culture to be unique and better than the other - this is not surprising as everyone does it; not just Jamaicans.

The Bahamas also host the *junkanoo* and rake and scrape music which is unique to them. In recent the tight relationships between the Bahamas and the Turks and Caicos have brought *junkanoo* to the Turks and Caicos Islands.

Because of our music a number of the well-known bands have been created; crossfire, burning flames and others - throughout Trinidad and Tobago and St Vincent and the Grenadines.

Music in the Caribbean is a combination of African, European and Indian influences, which makes it unique to the music heard around the world.

The Spanish music is quite different from the Calypso and reggae. I don't understand the music, because of its obvious language, but it was introduced by the Spanish presence in the Dominican Republic, Puerto Rico and Cuba. Spanish nations have now created Raggaeton and punta.

However, Haiti, Guadeloupe and Martinique music is inherited from a slow beat.

This is music that most of the English Speaking Caribbean does not understand, but it is well appreciated among the islands.

When dancing soca, it requires enormous energy and shuffle steps mostly involve a closed held partner. Reggae on the other hand requires less energy and less shuffling. This is also true about the French style music in Haiti, Martinique and Guadeloupe. The Spanish music varies and could have slow, medium and fast beats. Spanish music is mostly, salsa, merengue and bachata.

Our languages play an important role in our culture. The Caribbean Islands speak over 5 official languages and many dialects.

The Eastern Caribbean official language is English but most of them speak a local French Patois, Except for Trinidad and Tobago and Barbados that speaks English and have a local "Trini" and "Bajan" dialects, respectively. The Bahamas and the Turks and Caicos also have their own local dialects.

Cuba, Puerto Rico and the Dominican Republic main languages is Spanish with Latin dialects.

In Martinique, Guadeloupe and Haiti they widely speak French Creole.

Aruba, Bonaire and Curacao speaks a Creole Language called the Papiamento; a combination of English, African and native Languages.

Interestingly, when we officially accept Surinam as part of our region then Dutch becomes part of the many Languages spoken in the region.

Apart from our many languages and dialects there is a wide variety of other language from different parts of the world. The main languages include Arabic, Chinese, German and Russian.

Our languages are stemmed from African syntax and European Lexicon, which was use as a communication tool between the slaves and their masters.

Religion has also impacted the Caribbean islands. Some of the largest religious groups in the world exit and evolved within our region. Christianity is widely evident and has many other denominations. Hindu is also a growing faith especially in countries like Guyana and Trinidad and Tobago. Islam is also spreading like wild fire throughout the region. Many Christians in the Caribbean have been converted to Islam – again the twin island republic is at the forefront. A new religion called Rastafari is being recognized among the other religions. Rastarfari is predominantly practiced in Jamaica and other smaller nations, such as St Vincent and the Grenadines, Barbados, St Lucia, Grenada, Dominica, St Kitts and Nevis, and Antigua and Barbuda also practice this movement on a wide scale.

Fortunately, the governments of the Caribbean are secular bodies bearing no formal association with a single religion. However, I believe that most of our constitutions is intangible to Christianity, since Christianity is the dominant religion in the region and, moreover, the world.

Religion plays an important and significant role in the lives of families across the Caribbean. Parents use religion as a tool in the upbringing of their families, marriage and stability. An enormous number of schools and academic institutions throughout the region have close association with religion - most of these institutions use religion and the name of God to start their day.

Since the early times, Europeans' rediscoveries in the West Indies were reflective of men who practice Catholicism. From thereon, Roman Catholic Religion has spread across the Caribbean. The Dutch, French, Spanish, British and Irish were responsible for the introduction of this faith.

Christopher Columbus who was one of the earliest explorers to the region named St Kitts as Saint Christopher - a name derived from his patron saint. Similarly, St Lucia that is to the south of St Kitts was named after Christopher Columbus' own patron saint. Other Caribbean Islands were named after his own patron saint.

A similar contribution was made in the Spanish speaking countries of Puerto Rico and the Dominican Republic. San Juan, which is translated as Saint John and Santo Domingo, which is interpreted as Saint Dominic are also patron saints.

However, recent data indicates that the Protestant faiths have out numbered Catholicism throughout the islands. Although, the Protestant faith has various values and beliefs, it spread faster than the other religions through various denominations.

In the Caribbean there is an identification of almost every Protestant group. The citizens of the region engaged in a variety of spiritual beliefs - specifically, the Anglicans who follow the doctrines of the Church of England to the Christians that have merged the non-Western faith with spiritual beliefs of the Baptist and Methodist faith.

Similarly, Caribbean cuisines are the merging of many other foods from China, France, Britain, Spain, Africa, Netherland and India. This social continuity was handed down from the many many nations around the world that have gone to the Caribbean. In addition to this, the local population in the Caribbean has introduced several styles, which are unique to the entire region.

In essence, our islands possess local dishes, which are unique to them.

In the Bahamas there is a dish made from crab and rice. In Barbados they often cook cou-cou and flying fish. The Dominican Republic serves white rice and stewed red beans with fried beef. The Trinidadians make roti especially for lunch. The people in Jamaica like to cook ackee and salt fish. Breadfruit and fried jackfish is prevalent in St Vincent and the Grenadines. All these foods are from time to time served in other parts of the Caribbean on a given day.

The region hosts a huge amount of restaurants concentrated mainly in the cities. These restaurants are ideal for tourists visiting the islands and seeking a taste of the Caribbean. Cities around the Caribbean hosts many jobs and shopping centers, therefore, people would seek restaurants on a daily basis. Many of our restaurants are also situated at several hotels.

People from most Caribbean Islands eat the same kind meats – mainly goat, sheep, cattle, poultry, and pig. Some parts of the population eat animals like rabbits, Iguanas and agoutis.

Undoubtedly, our lives surrounds three kind of foods; foods from the sea, ground provisions, such as sweet potatoes, cassava, dasheen, plantains, Bananas and rice, and animal meats. This is true no matter where you go in the Caribbean; whether it is the Dominican Republic, Haiti, Cuba, or Trinidad and Tobago.

There many other foods, which the region enjoy.

The islands have acclaimed many local arts realism. However, the notion of modernity in the islands is sparsely a reality. Modernity exists primarily in Puerto Rico, the most modern island of the region, Trinidad and Tobago, Martinique and Jamaica to some extent.

In reality, some form of social realism is evident in the region, illustrating hardship and economic turmoil. To a lesser extend abstract arts plays a part of our lives where images are being used to display or communicate concepts.

Similarly, literature has formed our lives in some way or another. The islands produce many influential authors and journalists who have wrote about the political and social changes within the region. This part of our culture has bond us closer, creating an appreciation for regional stability.

Derek Walcott has been an outstanding writer, visual arts, playwright and poet for the Caribbean. In 1992 he won the Noble Prize for literature.

There is a need to give exposure to our regional artiste, writers, playwright, composer and the like, and there is no better place than the world stage. This is not only to display our cultures but an opportunity to gain recognition worldwide.

Growing up in St Vincent and the Grenadines, I noticed that Taiwanese brought their culture to our home. This is not all; we had to pay a fee to watch the Taiwanese perform their culture at the Victoria Park in Kingstown. They have an enticing culture, which remotely different from our cultures in the Caribbean.

I heard from many sources that the Taiwanese culture is distinct and fascinating and that they could not wait for the next performance. This is what we should instill in people's mind; force them to want more. If Vincentians could travel to Taiwan on a daily basis to witness their culture all over again they would, because of the lasting impression from the Taiwanese.

For recognition, most of our artiste, playwrights and more have to either depend upon record labels and personnel from England or the United States to promote their talents. There is absolutely no exposure at home, thus, the need to take it to the world.

The media is of major importance to our society. Its main goals are to showcase our authentic history of our culture - a place where artiste highlight their talents to the world.

The region is doing well with regards to this culture phenomenon. We have launched the Caribbean Media Network, which forms our television station, radio, Internet and Newspapers, allowing the Caribbean to demonstrate and express itself across a vast audience. The region also boasts the Caribbean Broadcasting Union and Caribbean News Agency, and lately the Caribbean News Network.

In this aspect the Caribbean is fully integrated.

There is a need for the islands of the Caribbean to develop cultural activities where representatives from all the islands could take part. Today what we are doing is to create our own cultural festivals in our home countries.

Caribbean Festival of Arts – CARIFESTA seeks to strengthen the social and historical bonds of the population it is a tool to create a Caribbean oneness through cultural identity.

Notably, the Caribbean Song Festival has been developed as a tool to integrate the Caribbean where Caribbean national demonstrate their talents through songs.

It would be a stunning discovery if the Caribbean introduces its own magazine, a medium in which we could showcase all aspects of our culture; artistes, Arts, literature, record labels, composers and songwriters. This would be vital to present our picturesque beautiful from across the islands. Therefore, we won't have to depend upon the major US and European magazines to showcase

With language, there is a need to learn and appreciate the other languages in the Caribbean. In some parts of the region there is a constant disparity amongst nationals about whose language is the best. In this capacity, we need to educate our citizens. I believe that more efforts should be placed in learning languages other than Spanish and French; Arabic, Portuguese, African and Chinese considering our backgrounds.

There is nothing we can do about religion. The basic idea is for us to respect other religious beliefs.

We should encourage international culture festivals across the globe and host regional cultural shows, which would display our lifestyles.

The food here is mostly, ground foods, marine and animals' meats; something, which everyone in the islands can be identified with. Instead of having twenty seven and more national dish, lets come together and make one huge West Indian recipe, which represents all of us and enticed the world to take part. This should be too hard to create, since the dishes are similar across nations.

Our arts, music and literature can also be displayed at these shows, allowing the world to see the diverse set of human quality, a variety of expressions and creativity.

There are many shows we could stage to promote the region. All of our Musicians, composers, writers, playwrights, artiste and other cultural personalities should team-up at these cultural extravaganzas.

What I have found is that people from St Vincent and the Grenadines purported that there music is the best. The Trinidadians believe that their music is the best while the Barbadians is convinced that there music is the superior. This is expected, regionalism does not exist so much between us. When we are integrated then our best music would be from the Caribbean and not from St Vincent and the Grenadines, Trinidad and Tobago or Barbados.

In the Caribbean we don't need different nationalities – we only need one nationality; we are all West Indians, or if anyone have a better regional name. In the United States people from New York are called New Yorkers; in California, they are called Californians; in Texas they are called Texans. When they face the rest of the world they are no longer New Yorkers, Californians, or Texans; they become Americans.

Another outstanding illustration is the Africans. It doesn't matter which country in Africa they are born; once the question is being asked where they are from, the only answer you'll get is that they are from Africa, it is for you to find out, which country.

Another good example is the countries in Europe. Most people from countries in Europe refer to themselves as Europeans, instead of Romanians or Yugoslavians.

As a matter of fact, the same could be said about Asian countries. People from China, Japan and other called themselves Asians. Middle Eastern citizens don't say they are from Saudi Arabia or Kuwait; they proudly said they are from the Middle East.

However, it is true that some countries still single out themselves and it is always the countries that possess a more stable economy. I have never heard a British citizen said he was from Europe. I could understand Britain's case; this country is not attached to the European continent and this is understandable. In addition to this, they have one of the best economy in the European Union and there currency is one of the strongest in the world, hence, individualism.

In fact, the countries of the west are highly individualistic; always seeking individual power.

Most people from South Africa will address themselves as South Africans. It is rear that they would say that they are Africans. The point I am arguing here is not that South Africans don't see themselves as Africans; the point is they mostly identify themselves as South Africans.

Altogether, the Caribbean situation is a bit different. Most countries within the other regions of the world except for African countries can provide for themselves and have sustained economies. The Caribbean Islands cannot sustain themselves on individual economies; hence, it is important and urgent that they integrate into one nation – the Caribbean, or the West Indies.

In this capacity, an anthem for the Caribbean is also relevant. Every island's anthem is the best, but a regional anthem is unique.

All of us have shared beliefs, values, customs, attitudes and backgrounds regardless of our country. We share the same climate – hot sun and rain all year round. The only major natural disaster in the region is hurricane and to a lesser extent volcanic activities and earthquakes.

When we carefully analyze the Caribbean demographics, there are many foreign nationals and ethnic groups. No more can we say that we are strangers when traveling to other Caribbean Islands. The Caribbean is so linked that we could travel almost every part of it and identify someone as a family.

During Eric Williams' terms as Prime Minister of Trinidad and Tobago when the Trinidad and Tobago dollar was par with the US dollar many other Caribbean nations migrated there – St Vincent and the Grenadines, Grenada, St Lucia, Jamaica, Guyana are some of the popular ones.

In Turks and Caicos Islands, there is an influx on Haitian, Dominicans, Jamaicans and Bahamans. The same could be said about the Bahamas where there is an explosion of different nationalities, such as Turks and Caicos Islands, Haiti and Jamaica. In the Turks and Caicos Islands there are also a number of nationalities which were hired by the government in various job positions.

In Barbados, because of the countries sustained economic environment many Caribbean nationals have swamped the shore of Barbados seeking jobs. Some of the big population comes from St Vincent and the Grenadines, St Lucia, Grenada and Guyana.

There is a similar situation in The British and US Virgin Islands and Antigua and Barbuda. In St Vincent and the Grenadines there is an influx of Guyanese, Cubans and Trinidadians, coupled with a few outside nationalities – Philippines, Taiwanese, Middle Eastern and other Asians.

In this sense, the Caribbean has become a closer family; various nationalities have inter-married and build new families.

We are identified by the slave era of the Caribbean and more so, by colonialism and imperialism. At one time or more all of our islands were either explored for natural resources or captured under the rule of British or French Empires. Spain had also played it parts in colonizing the Caribbean – thereby, leaving its remnants in Cuba and the Dominican Republic.

The Netherland Antilles have also makes its mark in our region.

With the presence of so many outside nations, our culture has evolved into something, which I termed as being unique. The way we speak tells of our past, the food we eat, coupled with other unique aspects of our cultures.

I love the cultures of the region, but I am not proud of the way it was handed down to us. Everything started from the time of slavery. All of our actions today were influenced by an outside party; we were forced to adopt pieces of other nations' cultures – nothing we know and do is original.

My careful assessment of our cultures indicates that our cultures are changing rapidly. Most people in the region are turning to an American way of life. A huge part of our population are listening to rap and R and B music, they dressed like Americans and commit similar crimes like drive by shootings and hostage situations.

Our diets are changing from sea, ground and animal foods to McDonalds, Wendy's and Kentucky.

Normally, our vacation is usually spent at summer camps and visiting friends and families in other Caribbean Islands and booking cruises and experiencing the snow in northern countries.

This is highly influenced by the advent of satellite and cable television in the region. Also there are many West Indians who studied outside the

Caribbean – United States and Canada especially those who adopt the way of life in those places, hence, the change.

Cultural institution are expected to plan and develop various cultural functions, which would showcase the Caribbean before the world.

Strategic venues around the globe and the Caribbean should be identified to showcase these shows and the entire West Indies must get involved.

Gone are the days when we promoted our home town, today is when we should display the Caribbean from a regional effort.

The benefits of regionalizing our cultures are that they maintain relationship and networks; respect for each other; encourage human rights and dignity; confer and shared leadership and some binding personality to the region.

Moreover, the values we share should act as the foundation of the guiding principles of regionalizing the West Indies, therefore, every initiative and procedure should be evaluated against these core values.

The worst that could happen is that each island holds the belief that their culture is dominant, more unique, or better than the next.

Successful regionalism through culture is no different from the other aspects; hence, we must plan effectively.

The leaders of our nations and other influential people – musical artiste sports celebrities and successful entrepreneurs, and educators should initiate and promote the notion of integration in the region.

In this capacity, we must take into consideration our various cultures and identity, especially in the case of Cuba, the Dominican Republic and Haiti – Martinique and Guadeloupe to some extent. To be honest, the Caribbean without a culture or difference in identity would be a monotonous one - it is what makes the Caribbean an interesting destination, hence, there is a distinguished relationship between culture and identity - one cannot exist without the other.

Our ability to successful integrate the cultural aspects of our nations is ranked at the top of our priority list.

I am aware that regionalizing culture is a tough road ahead of us, and it requires the right approach to combat the many perceived challenges.

We must thrive to be as selective as practicable in the integration process, which would produce value and eliminate unnecessary friction. We must start now and identify those aspects of our cultures, which would make a difference in our lives.

Amongst our cultures there are so many similar traditions and identity, why wait any longer?

There is no doubt that our nations would define their own culture and identity. Spanish Caribbean has different identities and cultures from French Caribbean and British Caribbean.

We have to also take into consideration the fact that many outside ethnic groups are living within our islands. These groups possess their own identity and culture, thus, a number of factors have to be determined; the socioeconomics, sociology and history of those groups. Some of these groups are permanently residing with us; therefore, we must consider them.

Interestingly, cultural change within the Caribbean and the entire globe is driven by the increase in mass media interventions, international commerce and, as evident in the region the rapid expansion of the human population, including other factors.

In our cultural change there are forces associated with social structures and natural activities, which are internal and two-fold in nature: forces, which embolden change and forces, which resist change.

Furthermore, social conflict and the creation of new technologies have impacted cultural change within the region. This is only possible by castrating social dynamics and encouraging innovative cultural models, in addition, stimulate social change; causing a shift in ideologies.

Despite the impact of the American culture in our societies today, acculturation was had occurred in the earlier centuries when the Native Indians tribes and other indigenous people across the Caribbean were crossed-cultured during colonization; hence, the culture of these indigenous people were replaced by European cultural traits.

Similarly, cultural change derived from the impact of war and competition over resources. A sense of this phenomenon is true about present day Grenada; the aftermath of the revolution. Also, during the fight over resources in the new world, these cultural dynamics were diffused, most evidently, into societies in Hispaniola, Dominica and St Lucia.

To successfully carryout this cultural integration in the region the theme for promoting this ideology must be clear and simple. The theme should surround the idea of hospitality and friendliness – all Caribbean Island is identified with these phenomena.

Thus, this plan should be developed in an effort to express our culture and identity to the world from any Caribbean Island. Programs should be implemented to showcase our way of life to the world. We need programs, which allow all of us to partake of cultural activities at the same time. However, to send the right message these cultural activities must showcase the Caribbean brand and not an individual nation's promotional strategy.

With a blend of a piece of every Caribbean culture into a regional culture the end result could be unique. The hardest thing here is to pinpoint cultural aspects. These multilayered identities is dependent on factors, such as our economies and institutions, and physical outlay of the islands, coupled with different characteristics, which exist in our cultures; ethnicity, language, religion and social classes. To move forward we must recognize all of these cultural aspects and understand the role of culture in regionalism.

~ **PART 7** ~

Education

Ideally, education plays an important role in the development of the mind, character and the physical ability of an individual. This philosophy is a fundamental need within Caribbean states; therefore much focus should be directed toward developing education within the region. From my observation, the region also has an obligation to unite all its resources to develop and implement a standard educational and research program.

The Caribbean possesses few scholars and educators, some of whom are regionally recognized. Some of the successful and outstanding ones being Derek Walcott, the Noble Prize winner, Dr. Ralph Gonsalves, St Vincent and the Grenadines Prime

Minister, and Sir Shridath Ramphal, the former Commonwealth Secretary-General.

There are many more educators and outstanding academia within in the region.

On the other hand, however, there are high illiteracy rates in parts of the Caribbean. Jamaica, the Dominican Republic, Haiti, Antigua and Barbuda possessing some of the lowest literacy rates. None of these countries, according facts, have obtained a ninety percent literacy rate.

According to trends, the reason for this high illiteracy rate within those countries is consequent to the weak economies and unstable political environments. Many children are forced to abandon school, because their governments are unable to provide enough jobs to citizen to sustain them and their families.

The Dominican Republic, Jamaica and Haiti are at the bottom of the literacy list despite the enormous schooling facilities present in those states. It is heart-breaking to know that Haiti has a literacy rate of 53 percent, which means that this country has more than four million people who are termed as illiterate. In the Dominican Republic there is an average of three million illiterate people and around eight hundred and forty thousand illiterate citizens live in Jamaica. These numbers should be staggering and stunning enough to engage our leaders to correct this issue before it escalates farther.

The other islands like St Vincent and the Grenadines, Grenada, Dominica, Barbados, the Bahamas and Trinidad and Tobago have higher literacy rates averaging somewhere between ninety six and ninety nine percent.

We all could agree about the reason for such high rates. These countries, especially Barbados, have more sustained economies and maintain a fairly leveled political environment. Moreover, these countries have well-planned educational program, which brings out the best in students.

Before we get to a higher standard, the youths throughout the islands must be educated, at least at the secondary level. We must develop a better education system, which would allow every student within the region equal opportunity to basic and higher education.

Education from a regional prospective is also cheaper than every nation fighting to educate the citizens of it nation. First of all we need more economical and political stability especially. Stricter rules and laws should be enacted to ensure that every student goes to school and do well.

Throughout the Caribbean, education should be funded and made free to all citizens at the primary and secondary level. In this capacity, I do not support free education at the tertiary level; however, it should be affordable, while special programs facilitate scholarship for outstanding students and for students that do not meet the financial requirements. The reason for such opinion is that many students tend to perform less well when education is free of cost-- people value hard work over things, which are readily available. More so, the leaders of the region must sustain a regional fee at the tertiary level.

I want everyone to get the point I am making about stricter rules and legislations. In this sense, I believe that the governing body of scholarship funds should be strict enough to allow failed students to repay any scholarship granted to them. Laws in the form of ensuring that every child receives her basic and primary education should be enacted.

This is a move toward regionalism through education in the Caribbean. This institution should be supported by the seventeen English speaking islands in the region, from Trinidad and Tobago in the south to the Bahamas in the north, with campuses in Trinidad and Tobago, Barbados, Jamaica and a Centre for hotel and tourism management located in Nassau, Bahamas. It is a profound discovery to see that the Bahamas becomes part of the Caribbean in this forward movement; also Bermuda that often see itself a superior nation to the Caribbean.

In fact, the location of Bermuda is not part of the Caribbean, and so is Belize, Suriname, Guyana and the other countries, which are not situated within the Caribbean basin, but these countries are still parts of the Caribbean by some form of treaty or signed federation.

Guyana has its own university, which mainly serves the people of Guyana. However, other Caribbean nations are able to attend.

Most other Caribbean Islands possess a university centre for students who might want to complete their first two years of study before going off to the University of the West Indies.

Some other islands have small community colleges, which serves those small communities and these community colleges are the step forward to enrolling in tertiary institutions across the Caribbean. Grenada has a regionally renowned medical college - the Saint Georges University, with extensions in various parts of the region including Dominica.

Not forgetting the larger countries, which include Cuba, the Dominican Republic, Haiti and Puerto Rico that have their own universities.

The University of the West Indies have produced many alumni, some of whom have risen to take top jobs in the Caribbean; Kenny Anthony, the former Prime Minister of St Lucia; Owen Arthur; Former Prime Minister of Barbados; and Wendy Fitzwilliam, Trinidad and Tobago Miss Universe pageant. There are many other political and diplomatic leaders who attended theses institutions.

The University of the West Indies has three campuses - one in Trinidad and Tobago, another in Barbados and the other in Jamaica.

It must be noted that many West Indians have been educated outside of the Caribbean – in universities located in United States, England and Canada coupled with other insignificant locations; Africa and New Zealand.

Nowadays, many students in the region are pursuing online and distance degrees from those universities and from University of the West Indies.

To encourage international recognition there is a need to employ international professors and encourage international student to the Caribbean. I do not believe that our regional education institutions are recognized globally; at least in the United States and Canada. I observed that well-educated Caribbean citizens who have sought employment in those areas, have to return to school before they can engage in employment in those parts of the globe. In this sense, we need to create some recognition and accreditation.

To address this issue, the region has to first integrate its education system, coupled with a focus on scientific research. There is a need to combine all of our resources and set one standard. Again the OCES member-states have always facilitated regionalism. This time it is good to see that the More Developed States -- Jamaica, Trinidad and Tobago, Guyana and Barbados -- have joined this regional effort. We have created CXC at the secondary level, and the University of the West Indies and the University of Guyana at the tertiary level. This is indeed a good start; however, there is a greater need to develop more programs and policy to finance and guide our education system.

Hitherto, it is important also that our education system focuses on programs, which would support exchanges and mobility -- a university program, which would support international exchange opportunities for many university and college students.

Conversely, the Caribbean must move ahead and start competing with the rest of the world through its education system. Efforts must be made to establish policy in this area to stimulate and coordinate research. The Caribbean must seek to allocate funds to finance Caribbean and national projects. Some areas that the Caribbean needs to diversify are geography, geology, oceanography, anthropology, archeology and other scientific research areas, including renewable energy to reduce our region's dependence on foreign oil; taking into consideration our environment. As a matter of fact, our region should and we can become the leader in this research area.

It is time for the Caribbean to produce doctors, physicians and surgeons, geographers, geologists, mathematicians, and astronauts that would lead missions into space. When are we going to have Caribbean representatives on an oceanography missions? When are we going to be on a geographic expedition? In this sense, we need to start looking at the big picture and explore beyond and enhance our regional capacities and capabilities.

The trend shows that the Caribbean is not making an effort to transform the education standards of the region-- an education standard that is compatible and comparable to the rest of the world. In this sense, I personally urge our leader to start investing in education and make our educational system a regional one. It is time for us to stop our dependence on developed countries and find a way forward for ourselves with their help.

Personally, I believe that Caribbean have to create international educational organizations that will discuss with these nations and convince them that our educational systems are no less practicable and effective than the educational systems in Canada and the United States. The British educational system is accepted therefore, our systems should be accepted, as our systems were adapted from the British.

This strategy will allow diversity within our education system and could, in the long run, decreases the amount of money we pay for tuition as regional students.

After attending international universities for more than five years I realize that international students pay as twice as local students there. At my university I paid one thousand dollars per course. The school I attended had enough international students to facilitate a lower tuition for local students.

In the United States some universities have three different tuition fees; an in-state fee, out-of-state fee and international fee.

The point here we have to promote our education system to the international arena, thereby, enticing the world to attend our universities.

First, we must extend our education system by introducing other faculties, which would attract outside students. At present our universities are specialized in faculties, such as Humanities and Education, Social Sciences, Law and Medical Sciences. It is important to offer more science courses that would accommodate more international students; in this capacity courses to be offered would be Geology, Astronomy, Zoology, Bio-engineering and other international studies, such as Asian, African, American studies. I am sure that many students are seeking a tropical environment in which they can study.

These courses are important to regional student in an effort to eliminate out-sourcing several positions in which Caribbean citizens have no skills.

I believe that the Caribbean should aim at developing technology, such as space rocket where Caribbean Astronauts and Scientists orbit into space.

In this capacity, more campuses should be constructed in other parts of the region to facilitate the influx of international students.

St Lucia has a sizeable population of almost one hundred and eighty thousand people and it is fairly developed with two airports, a good education system and good infrastructures.

Antigua and Barbuda is similar to St Lucia except it has a smaller population; about eighty thousand people.

St Vincent and the Grenadines would be another good location. It has a population of more than one hundred and twenty thousand people and developing infrastructures.

Aruba, Bonaire, or Curacao should be considered. Martinique and Guadeloupe should be encouraged to participate. The Spanish speaking nations and Haiti already possess some good universities – these universities, in my opinion, do not need to be extended – to facilitate these universities with high class lecturers, we must provide higher education starting now.

Grenada is blessed with a regional recognized medical University and so is Dominica and some of the other Islands. Extension of our university is located in Nassau, the Bahamas – a tourism and management school.

Universities in the Caribbean will also facilitate free movement of students. This suggests that any student to can seek admission into regional university and pay a regional tuition fee; we have only regional and international fee. A regional fee means that a Grenadian student, if attending a university in the Dominican Republic pays a regional fee and not an out-of-state fee. In accordance with this rule a student from the Dominican Republic attending a university in the Dominican Republic will still pay this same regional fee.

The region needs to be education not only for the job market, but in areas, such as teenage pregnancy, Aids and HIV, crimes and domestic violence, especially against women. The region has an obligation to educate the men about how to grow a successful family, as a huge number of West Indian men are leaving their children to strife on their own. Some children who are not strong end up turning to violent crimes and other hideous behaviors, unaccepted by our societies. There are too many unattended youths growing with no direction in their lives. The youth programs in the region are not adequate and effective enough to slow the challenges we are facing.

Programs in the form of spelling B competition, regional debate amongst students, regional science projects and many other programs, which the region seen fit to introduce, which will bind us together.

After all, once we are bond as a region, we must take our debate and science projects to the world – provoking discussions and competitions, which would improve our educational position on the world stage.

The Caribbean has Spanish, French Creole and English as it three official languages. Our education systems have already facilitated this integration move by implementing second languages in our school systems in French and Spanish, so that our students could learn about our French and Spanish oriented neighbors and vice versa.

I also recommend that these other languages should be taught from primary and elementary schools.

Notably, French and Spanish histories should be taught, so we have a better understanding about these nations.

An additional problem exists in our region. There are some ethnic groups, which we can't avoid from our school systems, therefore, were must include them in our planning. Their history must be thought in an effort to appreciate where they come from, what they believe in and, hence, will enhance the way we treat them. Some of the ethnic groups that exist are Arabic, Chinese and the Japanese. There is a small group of minority white race, which we must also consider.

The school systems in the Caribbean indicate that there are actions, which have to be taken when analyzing the difficulties we are facing from migration, globalization and changes in our demographics.

Moreover, the regional education success is also dependent on our social background of our students. Ideally, we would want to access the situation in diverse cities like New York and Toronto. They have successfully integrated their educational system – one that works for everyone.

We should encourage the notion of bringing our student together in ideologies and educational projects to make integration a reality.

We also need an equal learning opportunity organization in the region to allow all citizens to have equal opportunity to learn and educated them.

From empirical evidence in St Vincent and the Grenadines and interviewing other Caribbean nation, indicates that learning opportunity is strongly dependent on family background. In St Vincent and the Grenadines, this phenomenon is locally described as "Who know who." This happens especially, for students applying for scholarship to study at any regional university or abroad.

In addition, there are economically disabled families whose children do not have the opportunity for schooling. However, trends have shown that these are the students who perform and later become successful. These students often perform well at the primary and secondary levels – they rarely have the opportunities to pursue higher education.

After speaking to many successful West Indians, the reason for their success is solely because they tend to appreciate the struggles – students do not appreciate things that come very easily.

In reality, there is no education system in the world, which could facilitate equal learning opportunities, as there are many factors; cultural, economical, political and social, which prevent many opportunities for students. However, we must place efforts into reducing the impact of these issues on educational opportunities. There are countries around the world that have successfully accomplished this reduction.

In relation to educational opportunities the Caribbean has to educated people who have not taken the opportunity to attend school; institutions which gives citizens the right to start the learning process. Also, children, notably those who migrated to the region with a foreign mother tongue should attend an institution, which teaches young students to read. Toronto has a great program, which facilitate these students.

I am proud to be a part of this program for a year long.

Many of our islands are plague with many social issues mostly in the form of high level crimes. Those to note are murders, robberies, kidnapping and rape. These crimes are consequent of our unstable economic and political environment, but these crimes are also the result of lack of education within our society. People are who are not capable of reasoning to themselves. These people see crimes as a way of satisfaction for not being able to live up to society's standards. Many people see wrong doings as a way out and a prospect of maintaining a name among their peers.

Because people are lacking reasoning skills these victims are incapable of understand the importance of rules and regulations, policy and procedures, and law and legislations.

Research has to be at the top of priority. To engage in successful research the Caribbean has to develop some form of student exchange programs with the biggest researchers in education and sciences; United States of America, Britain and Germany.

Although currently, Caribbean students are utilizing their own resources to accomplish this drive, it is impacting the Caribbean in a positive way. Students are paying an enormous amount of money to conduct researches at various universities in Canada, England and the United States.

The Caribbean on a whole has been benefiting from educated people who have sacrifice everything to earn higher education.

Education should also exist in learning about the other countries of the Caribbean. The Americans and other researchers go to the Caribbean and researched the geological and geographical make ups of each island. This is something that we could do and ensure our own publications of the findings.

An institution should be in place to fund and encourage scientific research throughout the Caribbean.

In accordance to researching in the regions there must be research policies and implementation of research programs.

One thing I must advice is that there would be challenges as to who should initiate the leadership in the advancement of science and technology, hence, we must seek international co-operation.

Another area where I'd like to see much research conducted in the region is in the environment. We should develop a mixture of renewable energy as a strategy to reduce our dependence on imported gas. The United States is now developing ways to have this idea a reality.

Barbados has initiated this phenomenon – the country is now using a number of solar panels to power up homes there.

As it relates to the environment the Caribbean have to set further environmental policies. As an islander, the only environmental policy is to keep each town and village clean, by dumping garbage in a specific place for pickup and keep noise to a minimum – based on water and noise pollution. There is not a rigid environmental policy signed by a regional treaty – our environmental policy is promoted and informed by the Ministry of Health and the Environment.

Police are given the responsibility of ensuring that citizens do not pollute the environment and prefer charges when necessary.

Our environmental policies do not address the issues of destroying the ozone layer and destroying wildlife habitats.

Ideally, educational programs needed to be implemented on the negative impacts on all green house gases and finding solutions to fit these challenges.

The Caribbean is known for its clean and undisturbed environment, but if citizens are not educated concerning the environment and the policies to save it, then it is likely that we will lose this vivid theory of our region.

The Caribbean possesses the ideal environment to promote renewable energy mainly from wind and sunlight and even rain. There is a possibility that we could lead the world in this capacity; only if we have the right research methods and resources to initiate this direction.

The Caribbean should play its part in confronting global warning as we are the ones who have to face this increased earth's average temperature.

I must admit that the region has contributed to global warming by deforestation; cutting down and burning of vegetation for the purpose of agriculture and construction.

But there are times when the region is faced with contributor, such as volcanic activities, which are beyond human control. Dominica, St Vincent and the Grenadines, Martinique and Montserrat are threatened by active volcanoes.

Leaders throughout the regions will have to improve education facilities. More public schools at primary and secondary levels will have to be constructed also. A book scheme is priority for our students, giving our students the opportunity to access to text books, and access to more qualified teachers.

In light of this, we must continue to promote and facilitate an exchange teacher program. Back in high school teachers from the United States, Canada and Britain had gone to St Vincent and the Grenadines and other parts of the Caribbean and taught. The exchange program will enhance our crest for diversity in education in the region.

Another facility our school system should improve on is the library where students can conduct researches. Research libraries should include books, computers and Internet.

We have created integration in our education system by regionalizing Caribbean external examinations though the Caribbean Examination Council – CXC. We also have to globalize our school system by sitting external examinations through international bodies like the General Certificate Examinations – GCE - in Cambridge, England.

This is not entirely true about the rest of the islands, as the Bahamas have its own external examination; Bahamas General Certificate of Secondary Education – BCSE.

There is a similar situation with the Dominican Republic, Cuba, Haiti, Martinique, Guadeloupe, Some Netherland Antilles and US Virgin Islands.

To encourage our people to tread the right path our educated and successful citizens must act as role models to them. Many mentorship programs can be developed throughout our communities to ensure that all of our children stay positive, therefore, time must not be wasted on unimportant issues.

Success in education depends on a number of factors.

First, student must be given the opportunity to a firm primary education; this is the first eight to ten years of the academic span. The laws of the land should make this initial academic years compulsory. Teachers, parents and guidance, the state and other academic bodies should enact regulations and ensure that these regulations be carried out.

At his stage, students learn the basics of education and acts as a prerequisite for future courses. Without these compulsory academic years, students would not be able to perform during their secondary school careers.

Second, is secondary education, which also is normally the second part of the adolescence formal education. These years are also important as it determine whether one become academically successful. Without these formal years a tertiary education is not possible, therefore, it is important that teachers, parents and the government ensure that a formal secondary education is provided for students.

Teachers and parents alike have similar jobs to motivate the students, create an environment for learning and provided the basics necessities in life. On the other hand the government must ensure that the right infrastructures are in place for learning and make education formal and less expensive to pursue.

It is at this stage that students are provided with the basic knowledge of the work environment.

Third, is the tertiary level, where students tend to make their own decision on what school and field to study. In this post-secondary education most students study at undergraduate level. Few people pursue Master and doctorate degrees.

In light of this, one should know that it is impossible for a single government to provide everyone with the education at this level, therefore, citizens are encourage to motivate themselves and seek out opportunities rather than waiting on the government to provide everything. This is the importance of integrating our education system – the effort of lowering cost while enhancing education in the region.

Here the government plays a big role in ensuring that citizens are given equal opportunity to pursue degrees home or abroad, through scholarships and grants. The private sector also has to do its parts to ensure that workers are given the opportunity to upgrade their knowledge through higher education.

Other than training qualified teachers for the schools in the region at all levels, we also need to adapt the technological environment. Two things are important here; the use of computers and develop education programs through distant and online learning – these two factors complement each other.

In this sense, education and technology complement one another. With every piece of new technological innovation, training must be provided to ensure the adequacy of skills.

On a whole education enhances the economy of any country or region.

There are many benefits to be derived from education, especially from higher education. From a regional prospective, higher levels of education lower unemployment rates across nations, thus, this would decrease the poverty rate. It must be noted that these people pay higher tax, but they depend less on social-safety programs.

Having assessed the economic situations in Guyana, Trinidad and Tobago and Jamaica it only boils down to one thing – education. These countries have abundance of natural resources; bauxite, gold and natural gas to name a few and yet they are struggling to provide for their citizens. These are nations in the Caribbean that have high migration rates.

One of the problems exists here is the technological-know-how. We do not have enough resources and qualified people in the region to facilitate these positions, therefore, foreign workers and companies from international countries having to run these industries. The only benefit derived from these foreign investments is employment in some field.

There is nothing wrong in foreign investments because it brings employment to our nations and boosts our economies in many ways. However, the way it has been conducted in Jamaica, Guyana and Trinidad and Tobago is not favorable to us. These international companies basically runs the and partly own our natural resources, thus, they control almost every aspects of operations and profits. The biggest problem here might be the sending of profits to home countries.

As leader in this unique part of the world, we must seek ways to integrate our nations through education. We must equip our education system with creative learning and teaching in an effort to prepare our young people for future jobs and the rapid changing environment in which we operate. Ideally, there is a need to support the teachers in the classrooms and the institutional environment to facilitate innovative approaches to teaching.

To encourage students to pursue higher education through integration the leaders of the region must set high standards - not for individual islands but across nations.

Today, many foreign institutions particularly the United States and Britain are extending higher education to the region from the click of a mouse. Online degrees have also become popular in the Caribbean.

If International institutions see the need to invest into education in the Caribbean, why is this vision lacking in the leaders of these nations?

The University of the West Indies is obligated to set up distance education campuses around the region. There are many potential students who are confined by family commitments, who cannot attend university on campus; hence, distance and online education is recommended.

The most effective strategies, in my view, for economic development are regional focus and technology. In an effort to secure a place in growth industries and an economic future for the region our leaders must provide adequate training to the citizens.

If the Caribbean region is to develop into a knowledgeable community and compete effectively in the progressing one alliance economy top quality education and training are essential. In this capacity, education policy must be regulated by the Caribbean Community, and this body must set shared specific goals and shared best practices. Moreover, the Caribbean Community should fund a number of education oriented programs, which would allow it citizen to take advantage of their personal development and the potential economic environment of the region by training, studying and sending volunteers in different parts of the globe.

The Caribbean Community must encourage lifelong learning for all the citizens in the region. The region must also provide funding for this venture.

There is a need to encourage and fund adult education programs, specifically transnational networks, partnership, students' mobility and university cooperation. This will also allow students that are seeking to pursue education at the tertiary level and academics in countries from around the world to obtain masters degrees in our regional universities.

Similarly, vocational training should be one of our main focuses where young workers are placed and trained in corporations situated outside of the region – linking training institutes and businesses.

Ideally, it is important to make our education system comparable and universally acknowledged through a common Caribbean Community qualification body; providing an accredited framework comparable to the rest of the world. Too often qualified citizens of the region are being ignored with their University of the West Indies qualifications – purporting that our qualifications are sub-standard.

In addition, the Caribbean Community, in this aspect, is obligated to give the entire region equal opportunity to higher education and training, and other aspects of society.

We must focus on the outcome by monitoring education in the Caribbean from all levels – primary, secondary and tertiary. The governing body of our education system must be tough on the students of the region to encourage them to perform; performance, which surpasses the rest of the world.

We must do this if we want to be competitive.

The Caribbean has to equip its citizens with these relevant skills; our business and people would stay at home, and giving the many citizens to compete against the thousands of non-Caribbean citizens that take top jobs in the region. However, the aim here is not to eliminate entirely non-West Indians from taking jobs in the Caribbean, but to place a balance on the amount. In this sense, we are encouraged to take up jobs outside of the region – thus encouraging diversity in our workplaces.

With all these natural resources, these countries' economies should have been at the top of the economic hierarchy in the region, instead many citizens rely heavily on smaller economies to provide a daily living for them and their families.

The leaders for these countries should have recognized this academic need and work towards building this prospective. This is highly possible if we integrate our education system.

In one of his famous speech, Malcolm X stated, "Education is our passport to the future, for tomorrow belongs to the people who prepare it for today."

He also went on t say, "Without education you are not going anywhere in the world."

Furthermore, incomes earned by workers with lower education are positively influenced by the existence of university graduates in the workplace.

When we develop our education system we must aim to accomplish selection through capacity, quality, a firm self esteem and preserving our languages and values.

~ PART 8 ~

Economy

Integrating the economic environment brings many benefits. Our economy involves everything from a combined tourism sector and sports, a sustained political arena, a well-develop educational system to our identity through culture, to other contributory factors.

Most of the islands have similar economic systems – a mixed economic system, except for Cuba.

Conversely, many of the islands are economically crippled and cannot provide enough for the citizens that live there. As a result there is lack of modern and stable infrastructures. In addition to this, the weakening economies of these islands do not allow home grown businesses to escalate.

Guyana, Jamaica, Haiti, Cuba and the Dominican Republic are amongst the worse in the region.

I have had the opportunity to visit Jamaica and lately, the Dominican Republic. To be truthful I am not sure, which of these countries are worst off.

In Jamaica, poverty lies from the city and the way in which people live there make one wonder why the government is so inconsistent in assisting these citizens. Some people can't afford a house, therefore, they grab anything they could and make a shelter.

The hustling in the streets of Kingston turned me off, as everyone is trying to sell something, some things are legitimate ranging from home-made food to fruits, while some other things are downright illegal from stolen electronics to illegal drugs.

The Dominican Republic is similar. The thing that strikes me is the hustling on the streets. For every three hundred meters there is some selling food on the road side from roasted potatoes to boil bread nuts.

The capital city is swamped by many unemployed people who walked from cars to cars in the middle of traffic trying to sell anything they could place their hands on.

However, the country's topography resembles that of most Caribbean islands. There are many things there that I could identify with as a Vincneitan; the mountains are huge and these mountains are the beauty of that country.

As I traveled along I could see that the country had some development in the past. A big four lane highway, which stretches from Santiago to Santo Domingo and I believe, to other parts of the country like Puerto Plata. In addition to this, there are some overpass roads, which impressed me. The city possesses some high rise building, taller that those found in other Caribbean Islands. The shopping malls are huge by Americans standard. However, there is much evidence, which indicate these developments are suffocated, because of the state's inability to sustain these developments.

On the one hand, Guyana dollar is more than two hundred to one US dollar. This country's exchange rate five years ago was about one hundred and eighty dollars to one US dollar. This trend shows that the economy there is deteriorating.

I have never gone to Guyana, but it seemed as though this country had early developments. Because the country is plagued with inconsistent politicians and unsustainable economic activities, the nation's infrastructure and other developments are left unattended. Not because the government is slack, but its inability to sustain them.

Similarly, one US dollar to the Jamaica dollar is more than eighty dollar to one. In the year 2002 when I visited Jamaica one US dollar was equivalent to forty Jamaican dollars. Today, it is about double over a ten years period. There is an urgent need to fix the Jamaican economy, before it gets worse.

The Dominican Republic is also at the bottom of the list for weakest economies in the Caribbean. The Pecos is just under forty to one US. The weakened economic problem in the Dominican Republic has encouraged widespread prostitution. In the Dominican Republic it is not a norm, but away of surviving each day.

Not withholding that the Haitian Gourde is forty to one United States dollar.

In the region there are many other week economies which are quite similar to the ones mentioned above.

One of the answers in correcting this problem is to integrate the region's economies. The strong economies in the region could assist the weaker economies. Hence, no one is left behind or depend upon another.

I want to clear that the idea behind integration is not to depend upon another, but to work hand-in-hand with each other.

St Vincent and the Grenadines quest for development through an international airport has enticed many discussions concerning the relevance and the economic impact of this project. Discussions arise from both direction – some for and some against, and some discussions were raised from political prospective. Here, some argued that St Vincent and the Grenadines does not need an International Airport, because of factors pertaining to the country's market for tourism.

People also argued that there are three international airports – Hewanorra International airport in St Lucia; Grantley Adams International airport in Barbados; and Point Saline International airport in Grenada, within proximity of St Vincent and the Grenadines; therefore, there is no need to construct an international airport on that island. This is as outrageous as it gets.

The big questions here, are we going to work together as a nation? Or are we going to depend upon the other islands to provide for us?

Another argument surrounds the airport connotes the idea that the environment above St Vincent and the Grenadines is unspoiled by jet fuel. This is so disappointing and annoying to hear. Small and medium planes fly into St Vincent and the Grenadines and more so, larger jets fly directly over our islands. What is the difference? Barbados, Grenada and St Lucia are just moments away from the multi island nation where huge plane operate. If Grenada's airspace is spoiled by jet fuels, the same will impact St Vincent and the Grenadines, which is not too far away.

It is obvious that these perspectives are politically influenced and there is no real essence behind these thoughts.

In my view, excluding Puerto Rico that under the governance of the United States, Trinidad and Tobago is the most prosperous country within the region, specifically during the 1970's; its economy is struggling to sustain itself and provide adequate infrastructures.

During this decade of prosperity the islands was the home to a national Airline called British West Indies Airways - BWIA or B-wee as the Caribbean refers to it. This airline became the largest airline operating with the region and boasted many International destinations, such as Toronto, New York and London.

Many citizens of the entire Caribbean flocked in Trinidad and Tobago seeking jobs, which were not available back home. It is true that many St Vincentians have migrated to those islands during that prosperous period.

Today it is the opposite; many Trinidadians are leaving their nation for greener grounds.

However, in 2006 the company transformed into a new entity called the Caribbean Airlines when British West Indies Airways closed its operations.

The economy of the twin island state is not diverse enough to sustain economic growth, considering that this nation depends heavily on the exportation of oil to foreign nations. This economy is vulnerable to declining oil prices, as evident today, which began a decade later.

For many years after the decline in oil prices Trinidad and Tobago has been struggling to transition from an oil dependent economy to diversifying its economy - prompted drastic adjustments in its economic policies by the International Monetary Fund and the World Bank.

It is safe to conclude that other world issues such as the 911 and the decline in the Tourism Industry by global recession has hampered the country's economic progress.

The country's Gross Domestic Product is about twenty six billion dollars, but with one and half million people and almost two thousand square miles, twenty six billion dollars in adequate.

Today, the country's declining economy has championed the high crime rate there; encouraging a high volume of kidnapping.

Jamaica on the other hand is largely affected a dormant economy, which seemed to get worse. This country has a sizeable population and it is a fairly large island - by Caribbean standard. Its Gross Domestic Product is a mere fifteen billion dollars, a Gross Domestic product, which is inadequate for sustaining the entire nation after suffering from continuous negative growth.

Jamaica also is blessed with a few natural resources included fertile soil, lovely white sand beaches and bauxite. This country was reliant on the Agriculture Sector more than four decade ago then diversified its economy when it discovered bauxite. Jamaica began to trade minerals with the world; hence, the country sustained an adequate economy.

The land of wood and water as often cited by Geographers experienced tough economic times. During this period, the central bank of Jamaica has intervened in the market on many occasions, but it was not enough prevented drastic declines in the country's exchange rate. To date the countries exchange rate is almost a hundred dollars to one US dollar; a rate that many other Caribbean nations cannot imagine.

Mismanagement of funds could be the best way to describe the fall of the Jamaican economic instability. An economy which is so diverse, but cannot sustain itself. This nation is also confronted by large trade deficits. The Financial Sector has failed miserably and as a result the IMF had forced the island to make adjustments in its economic policies.

Because the country focused so much on bailing out the Financial Sector, it minimized the government ability to provide infrastructure and financed social programs.

On a personal note, this country's economy is too diverse for its standard of living. With such possession of natural resources, Jamaica should be one of the strongest economies throughout the region.

There are great potentials for tourism as that country experiences the most tourists' arrivals in any part of the region.

Jamaica has one of the largest emigration rates of all Caribbean nations. It rate is slowing up because of the visa requirements by other countries like England, United States and Canada. Even some Caribbean islands have this stipulation on the people from that country.

This country's Diaspora is one of the largest amongst Caribbean nations. It is said that "Jamaicans are everywhere." Each year, in the United States thousands of Jamaican nationals are given immigration status.

Similarly, the Dominican Republic, Cuba, Guyana and Haiti, which is have often labeled as the least developed country in the Western Hemisphere and one of the word's poorest countries, are amongst the weakest economies in the region. These economies are weak in the sense that these countries are incapable of providing adequate infrastructures and make basic amenities affordable to their citizens.

The Dominican Republic and especially Guyana have experienced declining economic growth over the decades. These economies are now focusing on controlling government expenditure and developing policies, which govern the day to day operation.

Similar to other Caribbean islands this country also has a huge emigration rate, which is being restricted by the implementation of visas.

In fact, the 1994 coup and the unreasonable financial and economic policies in Haiti have contributed the country's further economic down-turn. Consequently, the United States implemented sanctions on that nation, which further crippled potential economic growth.

Cuba is somewhat different economically. On one hand it is guided by a Communist regime where the government controls every sector of the state and on the other hand the country trade with international countries and open up its doors to tourism.

Cuba could be the power house of the Caribbean only if its leaders open the country for business and change it economy from the current Socialist principles to a democratic type economy. It Gross Domestic Product is fifty five billion dollars, which is not adequate for its population and infrastructural development.

Conversely, most other Caribbean countries are maintaining an efficient economy.

The dependent courtiers are maintaining annual growth with assistant from their dependent headquarters - US and British Virgin Islands, Netherland Antilles, French Departments.

The Bahamas, although its economy is heavily reliant on tourism, is also maintaining an efficient economy - on which is efficient enough to sustain its citizens.

Barbados also boasts positive annual growth; having one of the best sustained economies and standard of living in the region. Barbados' economy is more diverse than that of the Bahamas and the country's economy includes manufacturing, tourism, sugar cane cultivation and the country's ability to export goods to other parts of the Caribbean and international countries.

The Gross Domestic Product of that country is around five billion Barbadian and a sizeable Purchasing Power Parity.

The Barbadian dollar is two to one United States dollar. Many international countries do not have the luxury to have a two to one ratio. This is exceptional for a tiny Caribbean island.

In recent years, the country has joined with the other few top destinations that are welcoming more than a million visitors annually.

In the Organization for Eastern Caribbean States - the OECS, St Lucia and Antigua and Barbuda are the strong holds with Gross domestic Product around one billion dollars.

The other countries, such as Grenada, St Vincent and the Grenadines, Dominica, St Kitts and Nevis and Montserrat are trailing behind, but whose economy, although slow, have annual growth.

These countries use the Eastern Caribbean dollar, which is approximately two dollars and sixty seven cents to one United States dollar - the EC dollar.

Again, for countries with small economies, their standards are observable.

One can clearly see the gap between the economies of the region. I believe that if we come together and unite our economy that we can reach heights that no one can expect.

The Member States of the Eastern Caribbean have for many decades experience sustained growth. Not because all of the economies are strong, but the reason being that the stronger economies of the Organization for Eastern Caribbean States have assisted in keeping the economies afloat.

At age 35, I cannot remember a time in my life where the Eastern Caribbean dollar has been devalue. This same strategy can be adopted for the wider Caribbean.

In Europe, most of the countries in the eastern part had weak economies. It is the countries in western Europe that predominantly have sustained economies; Germany, Britain, France and other western countries.

Together these countries formed the European Union - the EU and presently, together they boast the largest economy in the world; about eighteen trillion dollars with the United States trailing. Together the European Union is the biggest exporter of goods and services and the biggest trading partner of some international countries like China and India.

Because of the unity, unemployment, public deficit and inflation has dropped to a minimum, while foreign investments are increasing.

I believe in a single market, which is evident in the region. The Caribbean possesses many organizations, which were established to encourage regionalism through economics. There are the Caribbean Community - CARICOM; the Caribbean Development bank - the CDB, Organization for Eastern Caribbean States; the CARICOM Single Market Economy - the CSME just to name a few.

As the way forward for Caribbean integration, the nations have adapted a common passport. The countries include, the Member States of the Organization for Eastern Caribbean States, Jamaica, Barbados, Guyana and Trinidad and Tobago. The dependent territories and the Bahamas Islands are not in agreement with an integrated Caribbean, therefore they have not signed the agreement.

These countries should take lessons from countries like Jamaica, Trinidad and Tobago and Guyana that thought they could survive on their own. I would like to stress also that these countries have far more resources at their disposal than the Bahamas Islands – they have far more diverse economies and yet their economies failed miserably.

I warned that tourism is the Bahamas main source of income and should another 911 occurs, God forbid, or another recession, they Bahamas will be affected tremendously, like other islands – at least, those other countries have other economic activities to lean to.

The Dominican Republic, Haiti are still seeking membership, but may not be granted signatory because of the share sizes of those countries. As part of the region they should be given the opportunity to become members.

There is a danger as it relates to the Bahamas. Not too long from now they would seek membership status either when the tourism Industry crumbles or when the Caribbean have make progress into integrating their nations and their economies.

If the Caribbean integrate their economies, it would be necessary to establish a single currency.

After reviewing the key single market elements of the CARICOM Single Market Economy there are many features which I endorsed.

I like the idea of free movements of capital, goods and services by eliminating all intra-regional obstacles, foreign exchange controls, and establishing a Caribbean integrated capital Market by introducing a Regional Stock Exchange.

Also, the notion of free movement of labor within the region is a good way to eliminating the barriers of intra-regional movement of skills and travel providing social services in health, education, sports and the likes; harmonizing the transfer of social security benefits and introducing equal common requirements and standards.

Lastly, is the right to own and establish business in any Member State without restrictions.

The CARICOM Single Market Economy is promoting many important projects, which would position the Caribbean on a competitive scale. Some of these projects include CARICOM Agribusiness Development program, Pan American Partnership against HIV and

Aids, Caribbean Renewable Energy Development program, and other economic stimulating projects.

Although so many integration strategies are being reviewed, there is not enough evidence that the Caribbean is integrated through economic activities.

To date, citizens are not able to move freely as purported by what is outlined. The only activity, which defines free movement, is the advent of a regional passport and using any form of identification to move from one island to the next.

The free movement of people suggests that citizens have the freedom to travel to other Member States where they take up jobs, live and study without regional barriers. This new venture also eliminates extensive administrative customs and recognizes professional and other qualified persons from other states.

The United States has the largest single economy in the world has joined with two other countries to create the North American Free Trade Agreement – an agreement signed by the governments of the United States of America, Canada and Mexico. Canada has the ninth strongest economy in the world and Mexico the world's thirteenth strongest economy. These countries are strong economically, with Mexico to a lesser extent, yet have identified the need to establish this trilateral trade bloc. Subsequent to forming this trade bloc, it has since become the world largest in nominal Gross Domestic Product by comparison.

It is my belief that the region could establish a similar trade bloc.

Instead of competing amongst each other in the Caribbean, it is important that the region operate according to the features of the single market, which we have put in place. It is time that we stop stealing from each other and create a single market environment. If the strongest economy regionalized its trade, there is a need for the Caribbean to do the same. This is not the time to stall the progress.

Similarly, a single currency should be introduced to the Caribbean. In this capacity, the Organizations of Eastern Caribbean States has long ago invested in this phenomenon with the advent of the Eastern Caribbean dollar. The more developed countries like Jamaica, Guyana, and Trinidad and Tobago should have capitalized on this monetary union after accessing their own economies and found out that their economies cannot be sustained without other economies.

It is long overdue to create a single monetary union.

The question is being ask each day by citizens of each Caribbean nation — they asked, when would the More Develop Countries going to wake up and join the good cause?

This question could only be answered when the leaders find the time to fulfill this vision that the Eastern Caribbean have created decades ago.

Currently, the Caribbean has more than ten national currencies.

Trinidad and Tobago uses it own Trinidad and Tobago dollar, which is one of the weakest in the region.

The Jamaican dollar is the national currency in Jamaica and it is far weaker than the Trinidad and Tobago dollar.

The Guyanese dollar is less than the Jamaican dollar and getting worse.

The Dominican Republic and Cuba use the Pecos and it is a little stronger than the Jamaican dollar and weaker than the Trinidad and Tobago dollar.

Similarly, the Haitian Gourde out-performed the value of the Pecos.

In fact, these currencies are the weakest in the Caribbean, but the Guilder used by the Netherland Antilles and Suriname has a higher value in comparison.

The power houses in the region include the Barbadian dollar - the national currency of Barbados; the Eastern Caribbean dollar – the official currency of the Eastern Caribbean, which is a bit weaker than the Barbadian dollar. The Euro, which is not an original Caribbean currency, but it used in Martinique, Guadeloupe, the other French West Indies – the strongest of all the currencies.

Belize also has a dollar, which is only one dollar and ninety six cent to one US dollar.

Again, my question is why are so many currencies in existence in the region? A region that is not even half the size of the smallest continent in the world, by land area, population, or economy has so many economic differences. The largest island in the Caribbean is around forty two thousand square miles and a population around eleven million people.

We should integrate our region through a single currency in an effort to be competitive. For now, the only competition we have is ourselves.

The European countries stopped competing between each other and they formed the European Union; the United States have seen it fit to stop competing against states and form NAFTA. The North Americans and the Europeans identified this move as a unified way to compete against the world.

The establishment of a single currency the member states should be legally bound to the monetary union. However, countries are not obliged to bind the agreement, and this is expected.

This single currency should be created in a way to produce transparency in prices of goods and services, establish a single financial market, low interest rates, avoid problems surrounds exchange rate and introduce a currency, which would be recognize world-wide, and a symbol of economic integration within the region.

The Caribbean Development already exists, which should govern our monetary policies. More so, the Caribbean development bank exists for the member states, therefore, it should employ a regional workforce.

I do not understand Barbados' situation when it comes to the single market - free movement of labor force. A regional institution is headquartered in that country yet the government is trying to stall the forward movement of the single market project.

Here I would suggest that headquarters of these institutions be located in countries that endorse integration.

This is current in the European Union; some Western European countries have not signed the agreement.

Since the introduction of the Euro it has become one of the strongest currencies in the world, value more than the US dollar by some cents. Ideally, the region should entice outside countries to adapt the Caribbean single currency. Montenegro, a country outside of the European Union has adapted the Euro as their national currency.

This is a lesson to learn – the Europeans have introduced it and evidence shows that it works; therefore, we have no excuses for not benchmarking the success of the Europeans and thrive for excellence.

To off-tract from the region, I believe that if the United States and Canada should unify, they would be an unstoppable force to reckon with.

In this sense, the region should operate under competition policy to ensure that no alterations are made to competition within the single market. The body that regulates competition should focus especially on eliminating cartels, antitrust and ensuring that mergers are sanctioned.

Budgets within the region should also be a focus amongst member states, which would develop other aspects of the economy including infrastructure, agriculture and energy.

A budget committee must be established with a representative from each member state with three to five members from outside the region, as one would expect disagreements about where development should take place.

The Agriculture Sector has to be set up with the aim of enhancing agricultural production, ensured adequate food supply, creating markets and ensuring affordable prices for consumers.

Agriculture plays a big role in many Caribbean Islands. At one time the Agriculture Sector counted for sixty percent of the nation's workforce. Not withholding that these islands produce agricultural products for local consumption.

Soils found in Jamaica, St Lucia, Dominica, Grenada, the Dominican Republic, Haiti and St Vincent and the Grenadines are similar – with rich volcanic typed soils, an environment, which is ideal for agriculture.

The budget committee must place more focus in developing the Agriculture Sector in these parts of the region.

I think that the Caribbean is wasting too much agriculture resources. St Vincent and the Grenadines is a prime example of that issue. In the mountains of this country there is an enormous amount of foods and fruits, which are spoiling every day. These foods and fruits; plantains, bananas, tangerines, soursop, oranges, limes and lemons to name just a few. There so many demands for tropical fruits and products – where is the vision?

Does our leader really take these important issues into consideration? Does the Ministry of Agriculture assess the importance and economic impact of these unattended issues?

I reached the conclusion that our leaders are too old for the challenging jobs ahead of them and that too many Caribbean Islands are too dependent on tourism.

We have too much potential to remain poor.

Let's look at a single nation's economy – St Vincent and the Grenadines that country I know so well.

St Vincent and the Grenadines economy is experiencing declining growth for consecutive years. When compared to other Caribbean Islands, St Vincent and the Grenadines economy is not significant. In this capacity, the Gross Domestic Product of that country in 2002 was a mere three hundred and forty two million dollars, compared to other islands such as Antigua and Barbuda, St Lucia and Barbados that have Gross Domestic Product over one billion dollars. St Vincent and the Grenadines economy is too dependent on bananas – there is a need to diversify.

This nation has the obligation to diversify even the Agriculture Sector. There are for more agriculture crops, which can be grown, other bananas. Just to name a few crops – ground foods, such as potatoes, dasheen, eddoes, coconuts, plantains, citrus, breadfruit and other home grown crops.

The competitive advantage is clearly in Jamaica, St Vincent and the Grenadines, St Lucia, Grenada, Haiti and the Dominican Republic. The focus should be on these islands to develop the Agriculture Sector.

The budget committee should also stress the need for the development of cross-nation infrastructure. Some countries demand different kinds of infrastructures, such as roads and bridges, harbors, airports sporting facilities, education institution including other facilities like satellite systems.

For instance, Dominica and St Vincent and the Grenadines require two into international airports to facilitate international arrivals of people, and goods and services.

Haiti roads outside of Port au Prince need to be upgraded.

In the Turks and Caicos the establishments of proper sporting facilities are required.

Recently the Turks and Caicos hosted the CRIFTA games, which were a success, but so much work had to be done for that one time event. These facilities should be in proper condition at all times.

Recently, the Caribbean, for the first time, hosted the International Cricket World cup. The nation government spent millions of dollars on upgrading their facilities. Some countries even built new stadiums for the tournament.

This is something that the region integrated economy should be responsible for, instead of individual islands taking care of this regional effort.

A satellite system should be implemented to eliminate the dependency on global satellite systems. More so, it would be an asset if we can tract our own weather patterns, considering the many hurricane threats per year. In fact, our location makes us prone to hurricanes and earthquakes. Some of our islands are dominated by active volcanoes, which we need to monitor on a daily basis.

This venture would be expensive; however, the islands won't have to depend on the United States for regional coverage.

Relative to this a regional economy would stimulate regional development. There are sturdy economical disparities within the region. In Guyana there is not a significant difference between the poor and the rich. The per capita nominal Gross domestic Product per is fifteen hundred dollars.

In Haiti the per capita Gross Domestic Product is under a thousand dollars.

The Bahamas ranks number one in the Caribbean with per capital more than twenty thousand dollars.

Other countries like St Kitts and Nevis, Barbados, Netherlands Antilles, Antigua and Barbuda and Trinidad and Tobago possess per capita ranging from ten thousand to nineteen thousand.

Some nations have per capita below tens of thousands dollars including St Vincent and the Grenadines, Jamaica, Grenada, Dominica and the Dominican Republic.

The islands of the region possess insignificant economies - economies, which are fighting to sustain the countries national affairs. Established companies within the United States, such as Wal-Mart have annual revenues much larger than many Caribbean Island put together. Even those companies merge at times. These companies merge mainly to reduce cost and use each other competitive and comparative advantage against their competitors. There is a lesson to learn here also.

In addition to this, the Caribbean possesses many underdeveloped countries like Haiti, the Dominican Republic, the Turks and Caicos Islands, Dominica and St Vincent and the Grenadines. This is where the region needs to establish a coherent and structural budget to bridge the gap between classes.

A combined economy means a bigger economy. With a bigger economy suggests that increased employment within the region is inevitable. Member States would have the privilege to move freely in search of jobs.

I believe this is the reason why many countries including the Bahamas, Cayman Islands, the Virgin Islands, Turks and Caicos Islands and a few other countries are afraid to integrate. High officials in some countries are purporting that they would experience an influx of citizens from other Member States.

This is expected to occur since they are more economically viable than some sovereign states. It is the same reason why Britain has not replaced its Pound Sterling with the Euro. However, Britain is a country with an extensive diverse economy and Gross Domestic product of more than a trillion dollars.

This movement can be controlled by enacting some policy and procedures indicating that that the free movement is structured for member states to move for the purpose of employment in accordance with the stipulations, which governs the employment of workers within the region.

Most Caribbean Islands have experienced positive growths recent decades, having enough to provide for their citizens - food and infrastructure. I single out Trinidad and Tobago and admire the enormous development there. From the twin tours to the massive Queen's park oval and other national stadiums, a modern city, a high level of sports, to the eight lane highway, which have over passes like those in the United States and other developed countries. The twin island republic also has the Caribbean most modern international airport.

This country's dollar was almost par with the United States dollar under the government of Eric Williams.

Similarly, the Eastern Caribbean, for decades, has moderately sustained economies.

Some of the outstanding figures included Grenada under Eric Gairy; St Vincent and the Grenadines under Milton Cato and Sir James Mitchell; and St Lucia under the leader of John Crompton.

Barbados also had good leader for most of its economic history with Tom Adams being one of the most prolific figures.

Jamaica also had a good economy and at some time in the country's history the Turks and Caicos Islands were governed by leaders in Jamaica. Under the leadership of Edward Seaga Jamaica became an economic giant in the region.

Conversely, the dependent countries are moderately assisted by their head states. The US Virgin islands and Puerto Rico are receiving tremendous assistance from the United States.

In my opinion, the integrated economy would influence modernity within the region.

First, it would stimulate the Industrial Revolution; creating changes in the mining, manufacturing, agriculture, the effect of the relationship between social life and economic activity, and the cultural conditions.

Furthermore, this single economy will create modernization where innovative technologies are introduced in all societies.

The integration through our economy is a sophisticated process, which requires enormous planning and development of strategies, but it is an urgent need for the region. It should be encouraged that we benchmark this phenomenon and get started at the earliest time possible. If we can't be original we could always copy from other regions, which have been successful through the integration of their economies.

This issue in economically viable, therefore, the leaders of our countries must aggressively plan this new possible and economic direction.

Some Caribbean scholars and citizens alike argued that the economies of too many islands are too weak to have successful integration. We must look at the European Union and take a lesson. The only countries in the EU that are economically vibrant are those located in Western Europe. To date, the EU combined maintains the world's biggest combined GDP. Is this a viable lesson to learn from?

This economic integration to take place there must be a free trade area, an economic and monetary union, a single market, a customs union, a preferred trading location and complete economic integration.

Moreover, for the region to succeed economically over time there must be gradual and more economical and political unity among nations. There must be some commonality between businesses in terms of customs duties and other joint ventures factors. Hereafter, there must be some proceedings for making economic and political decisions.

We must direct our efforts away from individualism and start thinking collectivism and commence building and combining our economies. All we are doing in the region is competing against each other and stealing the little we possess.

~ PART 9 ~

Development

It is expected that significant economical disparities would exist throughout the nations of the Caribbean; hence, policies and procedures are important in sustaining regional development. Barbados, the dependent territories and oversees departments, The Bahamas, Puerto Rico and Trinidad and Tobago are among the richest nations, per capita, in the region. The Eastern Caribbean Islands are in between and other countries, which include Jamaica, Haiti, the Dominican Republic and Guyana, are among the poorest nations in the West Indies.

This is the same reason that the citizens amongst the richest nations do not support this idea - regionalism.

With policies and procedures in place, and a committee that regulates this phenomenon and ensures that regional development is eventually distributed amongst nations.

In fact, there are countries that need urgent development than others.

Some countries gross domestic product – GDP is not significant enough to sustain the people of those countries. Haiti's GDP is a mere six billion with a land mass of more than ten thousand square miles and ten million people. The Dominican Republic GDP has a GDP of just over forty million people, ten million people and a size of eighteen thousand square miles. Some of the people in these parts of the region define the true meaning of being *poor.*

It won't be fair if I do not mention similar situation in Jamaica. Jamaica is a four thousand square mile island, with almost three million people, but a stagnated GDP of just fourteen million people. There is no wonder why Jamaica has a high emigration rate and a nation with some of the most hideous crimes in the region.

There are specific areas where the region needs development.

Our health care situations are some of the worst in the world. Most of the Eastern islands including St Vincent and the Grenadines have mediocre medical care for the citizens. Turks and Caicos health care is even worse off than that in St Vincent and the Grenadines and the other Eastern Caribbean Islands.

Improved health care for both citizens and visitors alike is encouraged within the Eastern Caribbean and Turks and Caicos Islands. Proper health care is not only needed for the millions of citizens, which call the Eastern Caribbean and Turks and Caicos Islands their homes. Hitherto, the millions of tourist that travel to these islands expect standard healthcare in the event that they need that service while vacationing in the islands. Many Americans travel to the Caribbean and they do not expect anything less than what is offered in their home states.

With respect to Aids and HIV, the Caribbean islands are less fortunate to deal with this horrendous disease, although the situation in parts of Africa might be worst off. Further to this, the islands have an obligation to find ways to ensure that healthcare and medicare to the citizens.

Practically, our communities have the right attitude and ideas about the pandemic disease in terms of setting up preventative measures, but there is lack of government reaction when it comes to providing financial aid to combat the epidemic. Moreover, there is also lack of government reaction when it comes to redirecting received funds to local organizations and ensures that these funds are being spent effectively and efficiently.

Some of these funds may be use to aid treatment of patients, although there is no profound cure for this epidemic.

But good health care exists throughout the rest of the Caribbean – Trinidad and Tobago, Barbados, Jamaica, the Bahamas, the Dominican Republic and especially Cuba.

Many Citizens from the Caribbean travel to Cuba to seek medical attention. Also, quite a few people especially from the Turks and Caicos Islands seek medical attention in the Dominican Republic and Jamaica, not only for the reason that proper medical attention exist there, but the reason that it is much cheaper with the US dollar exchange rates to these islands.

On the extreme, the Caribbean does not have the capacity and capability to conduct medical research to assist practitioners in their knowledge in the field of medicine. Certainly other nations, such as the European Union and the United States spend an enormous amount of money in research and development. Unfortunately, the Caribbean would have to wait until such results are released to assist local patients, and hoping that this information is released in a timely fashion.

It is a priority that the region boosts its health care, by enhancing the service by facilitating more advance technology into our hospital system.

Personally, I believe that the World Health Organization - WHO should play a more important role in ensuring that the Caribbean is given the same focus that bigger and developed countries are experiencing.

I realize that developed countries contribute a large amount of finance into the institution and that the leaders of theses states are more influential in getting aid; hence, this is the reason why the region should integrated its effort to become a stronger negotiating force, globally.

Additionally, affordable health insurance should be made available to all citizens across the region. To some extent, governments throughout the Caribbean have been providing health insurance for civil servants and in the private sectors, individual companies have been providing the care that employees seek. Unfortunately, there are many citizens who are not able to pay for insurance. Some of the reasons being that they are self employed and do not earn enough money to pay for such insurance or they do not have a job, which would allow them to pay and provide such service for themselves and their families.

It is important that the region develop such affordable service to its citizens and assist those who are less fortunate relative to their inability to pay for health insurance.

Infrastructure on the other, hand poses a threat to the development of the region.

Haiti is in desperate need of roads and bridges, community centers, parks and other recreational facilities. This to some extent is true about Jamaica and the Dominican Republic. The Eastern Caribbean once had this problem, which has been eliminated by improved roads and other infrastructure. The focus here must be on St Vincent and the Grenadines and Dominica that do not possess international airports.

Soon the airport issue would not be a focus for St Vincent and the Grenadines, because of it mega Argyle International airport, which is under construction on the mid-eastern side of mainland, St Vincent.

Barbados, Puerto Rico and Trinidad and Tobago are amongst the nations with the best infrastructure in place.

The islands have proper seaport – both cruise ships and cargo facilities, hence, the region only need is to introduce sea transport, which will move citizens within the islands and especially for those who can't afford the rising cost of flying; therefore, goods and people can move easily and cheaply within the region.

What is striking about the region air transport is that all the regional airline companies are going bankrupt.

British West Indies Airways -BWIA was the first to go. Air Jamaica, which was encountering financial problems for some time now, will be out of business completely. The only regional airline, which is dedicated enough to stay in the air is LIAT, which recently received enormous financial assistance from the government of St Vincent and the Grenadines.

But there is a catch to St Vincent and the Grenadines commitment to keep LIAT in operation. St Vincent and the Grenadines being one of the few nations in the region without an international airport; hence, without LIAT, Vincentians and visitors leaving and going to the multi-island states would not be able to travel. This is pure genius for the government of that country.

Again the Eastern Caribbean must be applauded for their effort. It seemed as though anything the Eastern Caribbean pursues is always a success, including their vision of integration through the development of transportation in that region.

My question is why couldn't BWIA and Air Jamaica merge and form a bigger alliance in the Caribbean Air Travel Industry?

The answer is lack of vision and business sense when looking at the situation from a developmental prospective.

The Caribbean Air Travel Industry could become so big that they could branch off into the rest of the world. Every other international airline has branched off their services into other parts of the world including the Caribbean. It seemed as though we are not ready to define competition and make traveling in the region a more affordable and competitive one.

While on the issue, challenges and development of infrastructure in the region there have been many cases of unsolved problems of sewers, power grids, water supply and telecommunication.

Especially in Haiti and the Dominican Republic there have been problems of power supply and sewage control to certain parts of those countries. There are parts in Haiti where there is no electricity; either because the government does not have adequate funds to extend services in those areas or the people are just too poor to pay power bills. In the Dominican Republic, many citizens there cannot afford to pay the power company; therefore, an alternative battery source had been installed in houses across that nation as back up power supply. A huge number of Dominican Republic's citizens do not have the leisure of twenty hours electricity.

The other parts of the Caribbean do not have these problems extensively; however, there is still a need to control sewage waste. Many islands, including the Eastern Caribbean, Trinidad and Tobago, and Jamaica still use latrines-an outside toilet, which sometimes causes air pollution within communities. This problem is decreasing by the day with so many people constructing modern houses. It is mostly evident in rural areas of these countries.

There is a similar situation when it comes to telecommunication. Some citizens do not have access to telecommunication unless they travel to a nearby town. This problem exists out of a couple of reasons. The first is that some people do not have the financial capability to afford this service. The second reason indicates that some government cannot extend such service to some classes of people.

As it relates to telecommunication, some Caribbean islands have signed years of agreements with international telecommunication providers to be the sole company to provide service. This has restricted other competitive providers from entering the Caribbean; hence, we have monopolized this part of our infrastructure. This means that whatever service charges were handed down; we had to accept as there were no alternatives.

Recently, this has changed and now the Caribbean boasts a number of telecommunication companies including Lime and Digicel, and Claro and Orange.

Additionally, most islands are guilty of demonstrating lack of rural planning relative to land development. In most countries urban areas are well-planned and executed, but for some apparent reason the rural areas land developers makes the decision as to who build and where.

For the past two decades, land surveyors in St Vincent and the Grenadines has been working diligently to organize lands into parcels and providing road and other infrastructures to land owners and developers.

On the other hand the region has an obligation to review it energy consumptions.

Of all the countries in the region Trinidad and Tobago remained the largest oil producer of more than one hundred and sixty barrels a day. Most of our islands, therefore, are huge importers of oil; the US Virgin Islands, Turks and Caicos and the Netherland Antilles are locations, which the United States might find attractive for refining and storing , for the same reason that there is a close relationship between the US and these nations.

If we don't plan around the impeding cost of global oil prices, this will impact the economies of the

Caribbean, as we are highly dependant upon oil and other energy consumptions.

One good thing to highlight here is that some Caribbean Islands possess the opportunity to important oil from Venezuela under specific conditions, one of which is at a discount. This regional initiative would allow these islands to import and consume more energy at cheaper rates.

Cuba also produce a small amount of oil, but this production is not significant enough to even export as this country consumes more oil than it can produce.

The largest US crude oil refinery in the region is located in the US Virgin Islands with other huge refineries in the Netherlands Antilles. These countries have huge exports to the United States considering that the United States are seeking alternative market in the importation of energy.

With the relationships that exist between the United States and these Caribbean nations, as a unit, we should be able to benefit from these relationships by pumping additional funds into these important projects.

Thereafter, the focus should be on Barbados and Jamaica that are initiating and planning these mega projects.

Trinidad and Tobago also export liquefied natural gas to the United States at great capacity. Similarly, Trinidad and Tobago is rising to the top of the world in this sense, hence, attracting and sustaining many foreign investments.

Energy consumption in the Dominican Republic is outrageous; many citizens, such as cab drivers and public car drivers are using propane to power up their vehicles, instead of purchasing gas from the petrol stations.

The world over is increasingly trying to eliminate the impact of global consumptions of oil as the sole source by leaning to alternative energy sources. The region must support the rest of the world in its quest to reduce the impact on global warming. Because of the cost of oil relative to Caribbean economies, I recommend that our nations make alternative energy a priority. The Caribbean is consuming more and more energy each day, due to the increase number of visitors to the region. In this sense there is an urgent need for the Caribbean to focus on solar, wind, tidal, geothermal and hydro energy.

Another Caribbean initiative is developing agriculture for food security. Ideally, most of the Caribbean Islands are equipped with the correct environment to pursue this development - the Dominican Republic, Haiti, Jamaica and the Windward Islands are some of the most popular agriculture oriented nations.

It is important that the rural areas of our nations be developed to allow the opportunity to insulate their local sectors; detaching from import surges and subjugate export prices.

I believe that the rules and procedures of the World Trade Organization are sometimes too rigid, especially developed to work against developing countries like those found in the region. These rules, in my opinion, should not only concerns trade, but how we treat each other - irrespective of cultural diversity.

It is also true that these developments are occurring on a global scale, however, we must develop and implement effective strategies, both national and regional, which would enhance agriculture and rural development across nations. More so, to lessen poverty and sustain food security in our region, there is a need to develop our agriculture sector. Trends across the Caribbean also indicate that most of the countries' rural population is engaged in agriculture; therefore, it promotes employment, encourages economic growth and development in those areas.

In recent times, the agriculture sector in St Vincent and the Grenadines accounted for sixty percent of the nation's employment.

However, the region needs to educate its citizens in the Agri-business Industry. Many people around the islands have negative images about agriculture and development. Investments in rural areas are discouraged and under-funded while urban areas are of focus and importance.

Additional, as a region we are obligated to diversify the Agriculture Sector by focusing on other crops. In the Windward Islands the main crop grown is banana, which has a big and potential market in Europe. From the islands there is hardly anything else being exported on such a large scale.

This sector, from a Windward Island perspective was once the *green gold*; is now struggling to maintain its initial success.

The Agriculture Sector in the islands are losing grounds to more upscale jobs as some people refer to them. The attractions are centered in the banking and tourism sectors. In fact, the Sugar Industry in some parts of the region has completely been dismantled with more focus on the service sector.

I can't imagine countries like St Vincent and the Grenadines are importing orange juice, or other items made from agricultural products.

The Caribbean cannot continuously import large sums of food, considering its economic environment, which includes the regions exchange rates to countries, such as the United States of America, Britain and Europe.

I believe the initiatives taken by the English speaking Caribbean when they establish the Caribbean Agriculture Research and Development Institute - CARDI, was a phenomenal break through. This institute was established to perform regional research targeting the huge challenges we faced concerning agriculture.

What is impressive about CARDI is the idea that each island is employed to focus on a particular area in the agriculture sector.

This move will allow for better research and development into specific areas.

Protecting our environment is another initiative we must focus our attention.

The region must enact laws and regulations concerning the environment around us. These laws should address issues relating to the ozone layer, noise, and air and water pollution.

Throughout the Caribbean members of the communities often use rivers and the coastal areas as dumping areas. This way of living destroys fresh water living organism found in these rivers, and to some extend destroying salt water creatures, by damaging the coral reefs, although coral reefs are destroyed in many other ways.

This image is not healthy for local communities and for visitors alike. It is understandable that we as local residents would have to live with these adverse conditions, but the visitors do not have to. This suggests that our standard of living in the islands is not environmentally friendly; hence, tourists would avoid the region.

Another popular act of degradation in the region is the constant cutting and burning of tree and vegetation for the use of constructing building or clearing lands for other infrastructure like roads and bridges.

Considering the topography of most Caribbean Islands, trees are important to avoid erosions and landslides in our communities. Also most of our islands rely heavily on agricultural crops; therefore, it is important that we are educated about the use of tree and the landscape. Rich top soils are removed during the process of erosion.

Notably, trees and vegetations are important in sustaining wild life habitats.

One thing I would like to highlight is bird watching. Bird watching is an important tourist attraction throughout the Caribbean, hence, the habitat for these species have to be protected. When trees are burnt and cut down for other use, living species have to move and search for other living habitat, thus the reduction in our bird species throughout the region.

Although not so extensive our region needs to build on equality and gender inequality. As we know equality emerged out of the belief in the injustice of myriad of gender inequality. This phenomenon was instituted to ensure that females have equal opportunity to develop their talents, as developed by the United Nation International Children Emergency Fund - UNICEF.

In light of this, I believe that women must be treated equally. In this sense, women are being paid less for the same job performed by men. To demonstrate this further, Women who are engaged in Engineering, pilot or mechanic jobs are being paid less.

The big question here is why such disparity exists? The leaders of the region must realize that encouraging and implementing policies that govern gender inequality is a way forward to greater economic prosperity.

Let me draw a scenario from the Middle Eastern and African nations. Gender equality is discouraged by those nations; therefore, women disempowerment has become critical in the development of these nations.

Furthermore, our leaders have to be minded of the need to encourage and promote the rights to equal protection regardless of gender.

Also, gender equality can be set up in a way that would rid the Caribbean of poverty.

Meanwhile, I would like to touch on human rights in the Caribbean. This observable fact was developed in the aftermath of World War II as an answer to the Holocaust. Arguably, there are not so many cases of human rights violations occurrences in the Caribbean, except for Haiti that has a long history of oppression by two dictators; Francois Duvalier and Jean Claude Duvalier.

Not forgetting the most popular the Cuban dictators who have for many years held the Cuban people under bondage. During Castro's leadership of the Communist states, the Cuban people were oppressed and demoralized; often being put into prison for their controversial views of the Communist regime.

However, throughout the rest of the Caribbean human rights issues have been controlled with a few complaints and cases about police brutality.

Conversely, emergency management is another observing fact, which we need to develop across nations; thereby avoiding risks by making preparation for disaster prior to its occurrence. It also involved disaster response, support and rebuilding communities after natural disaster and human-oriented disasters. In my opinion, I believe that effective emergency management depends on extensive integration of emergency plans and involved both government and non-government organizations. It must be highlighted also that our emergency response is limited to constrained economies, facilities and resources have crippled efforts.

Good Governance is another area, which the leaders of the region must develop and execute accurately, professionally and efficiently. When I say good governance I am referring to decisions, which characterize expectations, distribute power and confirm performance in our government systems and to a lesser extent the business environment.

Regional businesses whether regionally owned or owned by foreign investors should execute consistent management, effective decision making and processes, and coherence in policies and procedures, through evolved policies associated with internal investments, the use of data and privacy.

There is a need to measure the quality of governance in the Caribbean. This assessment should uncover the individual and aggregate indicators of our islands in areas such as level of corruption, political stability, legislation, efficiency of government and accountability.

This project should allow the governing bodies of the region to identify, govern and establish efficient, effective and accurate reform to combat the challenges, which may be faced by our nations; reform, which is adequately developed

The Caribbean is the smallest region in the world both by land area and population and the only region separated by water. Because of the size of this region it is easier for us to amalgamate; therefore, the only barrier is our leaders to come together and make it happen.

The United States is the world's economic giant and yet it merge with other countries whether it's military, trade or diplomacy. There must be something good about working together - the benefits are evident.

The Europeans, despite the varying make up of the economies in that region they have joined efforts to create the biggest combined gross domestic product in the world.

With patience I wait for that day when economic development in the region will enhance many of the region's slow moving economic indicators, such as poverty and literacy rates.

In this capacity the leaders of the Caribbean will remove all the barriers, imaginary boundaries and the little difference in culture and make the region a unit; a unit that the rest of the world wish they were a part of.

I also employ each nation's citizens to place all the difference and support the way forward.

Epilogue:
Strength Through Unity

Having possessed and established so many regional institutions – Organization of Eastern Caribbean States, Caribbean Single Market Economy, West Indian Federation and many more the Caribbean is on its way to full integration through its various indicators.

Achieving these institutions reminds us that progressively moving toward regionalizing the Caribbean. Although full integration is not present, I believe it is a good start. There is still a long way to go as the leaders have much work ahead in accomplishing integration.

To ensure that such target is accomplished and pursue these economical, social and political challenges; the heads of governments in the region must set up committees to investigate and deal with these challenges and strategically find solutions to fix them.

There is a need for the islands of the Caribbean to change their political environments. A steady political environment would positively affect the economic conditions.

Barbados has effectively led the way as it relates to politics and that country's economy. The governments of Barbados have always worked of the better of its citizens, hence, the country's sustained economic development.

Maybe, this is the reason why Barbados finds it difficult to join with the rest of the region in promoting regionalism.

Also, individualism must be wiped from our minds – one cannot survive alone in this modern world; one will always need the other person to reply on. Here we must think comparative and competitive advantages. Ideally, some islands possess resources, which are not found in other parts of the region, therefore the need to integrate.

There are too much efforts spent on individual countries rather than thinking collectively. There are many benefits to be derived from collectivism.

The main philosophical underpinning of collectivism is to be associated with holism where the whole is viewed as being greater than the sum of the parts, rather than achieving individual goals.

In this sense collectivism is often referred to corporatism suggesting that a group of interrelated parts - economical, political and social organizations in the form of ethnic, religious, business, military, farmer groups join together to a united governing body to establish policies and procedures to satisfy various groups within the body. With collectivism all parts must be functioning in the interest of the system to reduce conflicts amongst member states.

When the Europeans could not produce their own sugar, they fought amongst each other to gain control over islands in the region that have potential for sugar crops. In doing so, they had no reason to spend money in importing sugar from foreign lands.

Trinidad and Tobago possess natural gas, which is not found anywhere else in the Caribbean.

St Vincent and the Grenadines is blessed with nature trails, which does not exist in countries like Barbados and Antigua and Barbuda.

To survive politically, socially and economically the islands need each other leadership, resources and technology to be effective, efficient and competitive.

Political survival is reliant on the support of a successful coalition of citizens who welcome the change. Political survival in its regional terms implies that leaders must be willing to compromise to get things done. It is seen as a system and that all parts of the system are as important to the other.

Moreover, it is proven that political powers within a larger unit create efficiencies of scales for the region. It extensively encourages decentralization where the citizens of the regions are closely involved in problem-solving and decision making; therefore, it allows the citizens to realize how important they are in the development of the region; hence, better corporation in institutionalizing the various sectors within the system.

Furthermore, the region has an obligation to educate its people about the new direction in which the region is heading and to establish institutions to link our unique nations together. The Caribbean television network, regional radio stations and other media like the news media should be used to help promote the integration effort.

Parents, governments and organizations must work closely with each other to see that all citizens are educated. Government must provide the basic needs at the primary and secondary levels and must make scholarships and other funds available to those at the tertiary level. Companies and organizations alike should educate their workers through scholarship funds and regular courses to keep their workers abreast of the working environment. Parent are obligated to ensure that their children understand the need and importance of education and guide them along the way.

It is my view that more technological oriented studies should be introduced to the region - computer science, media, engineering, and other courses and faculties, which would position us in advanced fields.

I am sure that there are West Indians who have dreamt about traveling to space - these are areas where we need to focus our education. There are opportunities to explore more of the world and what it has to offer. Going to the moon or space is not Russian, European, Asian, or a North American dream it is also for those who want to make it a reality.

The region has been trying so hard to integrate its resources for decades now; the initial attempt was in 1958 when they form the West Indian Federation. This institution was introduced to seize Britain and other European control over the region. This failed early in the implementation stage.

This failure suggests that we are not planning effectively. Our strategies are not working therefore; it is recommended that the leaders of the region consult the European Union and the United States. Regional leaders and committees should benchmark these two regions that have successfully integrated in many forms.

In addition, the citizen of our nations should be included in an effort to gain their approval and help win others to encourage the movement.

One thing I have learnt about change is that it does not happen overnight, therefore, time have to be allotted to change people. The change should be well communicated and the benefits shown to people.

Consequently, the implementation and procedures must be discussed with those to be changed.

It is expected that there are people who would resist this change; hence, resistance to change should be properly managed. People who welcome the change should be used to win over the people who resist such change.

I realized that some of islands see themselves as the superiors, and I am aware that many of our islands have their own internal problems.

In light of this, I am forced to write this book not because the region has failed to integrate on many fronts, but to stir up the need for the region to integrate and to share what I know to the leaders of our nations. More so, the aim here is to try to influence the mind of the people living in the region. This strategy has to reach West Indians like they have never been reached before. Therefore, I will seek to encourage my thoughts through a simple book entitled, Regionalism: The Caribbean prospective.

This book will take you back to the time when the Caribbean first existed – long before Christopher Columbus came to our New World.

It encompasses the colonial period and describes the modern territories of the region and why its nations behave the way they are today.

Different aspects of the region are discussed; explaining how the regions should link its resources and the benefits to be derived.

The region is linked by many institutions but only a small fraction of the region's activities are integrated.

The countries of the Organization of Eastern Caribbean States must be recognized for their effort in creating this inter-governmental organization, that still in operation today. Currently, this harmonization is working well for its member states this is where the rest of the region should start from by gaining membership – countries including Jamaica, Trinidad and Tobago, the Bahamas and other non-member states should join.

I am not happy with the slow progress we are making in integrating the region. It is hard to sit back and see nothing is being done about associating our nations that are struggling in every aspect.

These challenges have encouraged me to get involved in political, social and economical debates across the region in an effort of influence the idea of a one Caribbean region.

My strategy is to first get involved in local politics in my hometown of St Vincent and the Grenadines – running for office of the prime minister and, thereafter, seek prominence in a strategic plan, which effectively and efficiently integrate the Caribbean.

My message should be clear through this book so when the time comes for me to lead the way though integration of the West Indies, the people would already know of my intentions.

Personal quotes:

~ "You cannot please people by doing what they want; you please them by doing the right thing."

~ "One minute of bickering is a lifetime short of progress."

~ "To stay neutral and moving forward, you must support good governance and constructively criticize bad decision making regardless of party."